SOME GAVE ALL

FORGOTTEN OLD WEST LAWMEN
WHO DIED WITH THEIR BOOTS ON

SOME GAVE ALL

FORGOTTEN OLD WEST LAWMEN
WHO DIED WITH THEIR BOOTS ON

J.R. SANDERS

MOONLIGHT MESA
ASSOCIATES

SOME GAVE ALL
FORGOTTEN OLD WEST LAWMEN WHO DIED WITH THEIR BOOTS ON

PRINTED IN THE UNITED STATES OF AMERICA

Published by:

Moonlight Mesa Associates, Inc.
Wickenburg, AZ

www.moonlightmesaassociates.com
orders@moonlightmesaassociates.com

ISBN: 978-1-938628-23-8

LCCN: 2013952334

Vendor Queries Welcome

DEDICATION

For Michael Crain and Jeremiah MacKay – recent inductees into a grim but proud fraternity. If only it could be closed to future membership. If only.

TABLE OF CONTENTS

Foreword
Acknowledgments
Introduction

FOREWORD

In yesteryear, and it really is no different today, most law officers were unsung as they went about their often thankless jobs. Enforcing town and county ordinances, putting the drunk and disorderly behind bars, responding to domestic disputes, testifying in courtrooms and doing endless paperwork – such things were the usual order of the officer's working day, even in the shoot-'em-up era known as the Wild West. But every so often the seemingly mundane could turn insane. Tempers would flare, bullets would fly, and people would die. Sometimes those people were marshals, sheriffs, constables, detectives and other badge wearers. In California alone during its first fifty years of statehood (1850–1900), fifty-six officers died by gunfire. Getting shot down in the line of duty almost guaranteed a lawman a write-up in the local papers and maybe beyond if the circumstances were dramatic enough. Lawmen who died with their boots on would be mourned, of course, possibly praised for their months or years of community service, and lauded for their heroic if ultimately unsuccessful final actions. It was a hell of a way to get attention, though, and the attention spans of communities, territories, states and nations don't often span many years. Late lawmen are forgotten soon enough, sometimes much quicker than the bad men who made them "late" by cutting them down before their time.

Diligent researcher J.R. Sanders has dug up ten intriguing stories about fallen and mostly forgotten lawmen (fourteen such officers, as one true tale involves multiple deaths) in the American West between 1879 and 1910. He suggests that the act of pinning on a badge is heroic in itself and that we should remember all lawmen who served honorably, including those who died with their boots off. Of course, even if we consider only the lawmen of Wild West days, we never could know all their names, and to tell all their individual stories would not be possible even if Mr. Sanders penned a hundred sequels. For now we must settle for the chosen few. Fortunately J.R. has chosen wisely.

We have Humphrey R. Symons, a man who gave up mining for the seemingly safer work of keeping the peace and became the first Nevada lawman killed while responding to domestic abuse. We have Deputy Sheriff Cash Hollister, who was said to be a terror to evildoers in Kansas but was shot down by a two-timing scoundrel who had run off with a farmer's daughter. We have Hal Gosling, a fearless and genial U.S. Marshal whose errors in judgment while escorting two prisoners on a Texas train led to three deaths, including his own. We have Detective J.W. Gilley, who was in a courtroom when mortally wounded in a stabbing, yet managed to pull out his revolver and fire four times at his attacker. And that's just in the first four chapters. In later chapters we have City Marshal James F. Isbell of Bells, Texas; Tehama County (California) Sheriff J.J. Bogard; Alameda County (California) lawmen Dan Cameron, Joseph Lerri, Charles White, George Woodsum and Gustave Koch, who all died in a single, explosive incident; Platte County (Missouri) Sheriff John Dillingham; Special Agent David Calhoun of the Atchison, Topeka & Santa Fe Railway Police; and City Marshal John Rennix of New Castle, Colorado.

For a quarter century I have been working for a magazine that features articles about outlaws and lawmen of the Old West in every issue. Still, I never before knew about (or else I had forgotten about) all but two or three of Mr. Sanders' chosen heroes. Maybe I'll remember some of these names now. If not, I'll certainly remember some of their stories. Other readers will no doubt do better than me, because, without a doubt, J.R. Sanders tells these stories with flair, bringing out the drama in the lives and deaths of some of the countless Western lawmen worth knowing.

Gregory Lalire, Editor of *Wild West* Magazine
Leesburg, Virginia, 2013

Acknowledgments

This book was made possible by the assistance of a number of individuals and organizations. Chief among these is my wife Rose, whose patience and loving support have made all the difference in this project, as they do in all things. Special thanks go also to *Wild West* magazine editor Greg Lalire for kindly agreeing to write a foreword, and for his professional support through the years.

The following is a list of other people and groups without whose help this book would not exist. Any omissions are my oversight alone, and I apologize in advance.

Elaine Bay, Grayson County (TX) GenWeb

Denver Public Library, Western History/Genealogy

John A. Dillingham

Sarah Gilmor, History Colorado

Doug Gist, Silver State National Police Officers Museum

Richard L. Henry

Micheal Hodges, Texas Press Association

Kansas City (MO) Public Library

Sgt. Emmett Lockridge, Kansas City (KS) Police Department

Grace McEvoy, Austin History Center, Austin Public Library

Lorraine and William J. McNeal, New Castle (CO) Historical Society

Elizabeth C. Moore, Nevada State Library and Archives

Nancy Sherbert, Kansas State Historical Society

INTRODUCTION

"Show me a hero, and I will write you a tragedy"
F. Scott Fitzgerald

Once upon a time, in the ever more distant past, heroes were grand, larger-than-life figures: The Oxford English Dictionary gives its earliest definition of them as "men of superhuman strength, courage or ability, favored by the gods." More recently the dictionary has broadened – some would say lowered – the definition to include "a man admired and venerated for his achievements and noble qualities." In 1943, Gerald White Johnson made the cynical claim in his *American Heroes and Hero Worship* that "heroes are created by popular demand, sometimes out of the scantiest materials or none at all." A bold statement at the height of the Second World War, but it makes the point that we Americans are a people enamored with heroes and are not always particular on whom we fasten the label. This has never been truer than the present time. Today's "heroes" are more often sports figures, entertainers and other "celebrities", and even the latter term has been diluted to include people of dubious or manufactured notoriety – think reality television or YouTube. Heroes – in the classic sense – do exist of course, but they are rare. Most of us are little more than the sum of our flaws, and so in the day-to-day, with no other heroes in sight, we're willing to settle.

But it takes – or ought to – more than fame to make a true hero. In seeking them, we'd do better to fall back toward the earlier definitions, focusing on individuals who've faced real dangers and made real sacrifices, humbly and selflessly. While our hunger for heroes leads us to search in unlikely places, we often overlook them in likely ones. Among those tasked with protecting the public, such as our military, firefighters, and police officers, can be found examples of heroism every day. But these often get little play in the realm of popular opinion, particularly in the case of police officers. Our national mindset causes us to resent authority, and so Americans have always had a love/hate relationship with their police. We'll mourn a fallen officer or cheer one who's put his or her life on the line and saved the day, but with the next breath curse the cop who gave us a traffic ticket. We can fail to recognize that simply pinning on a badge is, in the traditional sense, a heroic act. In few other professions do its practitioners leave for work each day with a reasonable doubt of returning home. And while a given officer won't necessarily perform Homeric acts daily, the inescapable fact is that peace officers are paid not so much for what they do as for what they're *willing* to do.

This was at least as true in the latter 19th and the early 20th centuries, when our country was still pushing westward into mostly unsettled areas, and civilized society, as we understood it, was struggling to take firm root. Yet consider Wyatt Earp, Bat Masterson and Wild Bill Hickok. They are legends, icons of the Old West. Nearly everyone would recognize the names, and most could recite a few details, at least, of the lives of such celebrated figures. Earp, in particular, has inspired a devoted, near cultic interest to this day. He's a uniquely polarizing figure among Western aficionados, either reviled or revered: Earpies worship him, Clantonistas hang him in effigy, but no one ignores him. Debates over his doings still incite such vitriol as threatens to make the O.K. Corral fracas – the spark of the Earpen legend – look like a schoolyard scuffle. Yet the inconvenient truth is that Earp's repute as a steely-eyed upholder of law and order rests on thirty seconds spent standing alongside his brothers and best pal in a weed-choked vacant lot. Brave, courageous and bold? Certainly. Heroic? Depends which side of the dispute you believe.

This is not to make light of Earp's genuine accomplishments – whatever they were – nor of Hickok's and Masterson's. Though their tin stars shine a bit less brightly in the firmament of Old West lore they, too, have their following, and rightly so. Each (yes, even Earp) is entitled to his status as a genuine celebrity, whether or not a hero, of the Wild West. Still, two facts common to all three men must be borne in mind. First, that their fame rests primarily upon their exploits as lawmen, though each pursued that vocation sporadically, and none for more than a cumulative fistful of years. Second, that each is remembered today not so much for the extraordinary deeds he did as for the fact that those deeds were recorded – often *distorted* – for a popular audience. Each benefited from a biographer who carefully crafted his exploits into the stuff of legend. In Earp's case, the biography was posthumous, and his legend given further luster by his devoted widow. Hickok died young, murdered in his prime, having had few years to savor his celebrity. Masterson alone was able to enjoy, and actively contribute to, his exalted status until well into his senior years, and another century.

That said, it's not this book's purpose to denigrate or cast doubt upon the reputations of such men. Better writers and historians can, and have, delved into their careers and separated the grains of historical truth from the chaff. But while barrels of ink have been spilled over Earp, et al, many other Old West "law dogs" who engaged in exploits equal to those of their renowned contemporaries are little, if at all, known today. They've been overlooked, forgotten, or, in the parlance of their day, "disremembered" largely for one simple reason. They died in the line of duty, lives and careers cut short and any chance at lasting glory buried with them. Their brave sacrifices earned them only a few lines (a column if they were lucky) in the newspaper of the day, perhaps a page or two in a long-forgotten book, or a paragraph in more recent accounts. Beyond this, they've been swept into history's dustbin. And any one of them, given the chance, could have – and would have – stood shoulder-to-shoulder with the "heroes" of Western legend.

This book's purpose, then, is twofold. First it seeks to pay tribute. It is a humble attempt to give a few brave souls a bit of long overdue recognition for their sacrifices. Secondly, its purpose is to acquaint readers with true tales as exciting and engaging as any told about the usual suspects who, after all, have already been the heroes of countless dime novels, books, films and radio and television shows.

Sadly, this volume is far from all-inclusive. The vast honor roll of American peace officers who have made the ultimate sacrifice (starting with Robert Forsyth in 1789) could not be contained in a single book, nor with any detail in a hundred such books. Rather, this is a small sampling, focusing on peace officers in the Western states. Cases covered here are confined to the Old West period, a subjective term that for our purposes includes the first decade of the 20th century, when horseback travel, in the West, was still the norm. These accounts give great emphasis to contemporary newspaper reports, which provide some of the most lively and colorful, if not always reliable, recording of events. In so far as possible, such sources have been fact-checked to insure accuracy. The officers included here represent varying agencies and ranks, from various states and all across the law enforcement spectrum. As the great Kansas statesman of the day, John James Ingalls, once remarked, "In the democracy of the dead, all men are at last equal. There is neither rank nor station nor prerogative in the republic of the grave."

Actually, there is a third object of *Some Gave All* – to highlight the lot of early law enforcement officers, who functioned before modern innovation and organization and without, in most cases, any well-structured system of support. Resources today's officers take for granted would have been welcome luxuries to these men. Still, those interested in, or employed in, modern law enforcement will find plenty of parallels with police work as it is today. Modern officers will find many methods and tactics these men used antiquated, maybe even foolhardy, but as they cringe it's important to consider these things in the context of the times. Old West lawmen had no training academies, nor even training officers, as we know them. They were mostly underpaid, undertrained, understaffed and undersupported.

They were all too often forced to work without backup, and had no ready, efficient means to summon help even had it been available. Nothing here is meant to judge or malign the men or their methods; what seems "common sense" to today's officers these fellows learned through trial and error. The frontier lawman's job knowledge and savvy were hard won, and often an example of the adage that good judgment comes from experience, and that most of that comes from bad judgment. In law enforcement, bad judgment sometimes kills, so the fact that these officers willingly faced such hazards with such scanty resources makes them all the more heroic.

As too often happens today, some of the officers chronicled here died performing what seem – by Wild West standards, anyway – mundane duties. In contrast to the popular image of posses galloping after bad men, or dusty street fights with bank robbers, they were performing everyday functions like transporting prisoners, enforcing minor statutes, intervening in domestic disputes, or appearing in court – precisely the sort of common duties modern police trainers caution against viewing as "routine." On the topic of courts, another enduring myth shaped by a century-plus of novels, films and television shows is that Old West justice was ever swift and sure. Readers will likely be amazed at the courtroom proceedings that followed many of these cases; they might have been lifted from today's headlines. After all, the same basic legal framework was in place when John Pritchard was tried for killing Humphrey Symons as when O.J. Simpson stood trial for a double murder over a century later. It shouldn't be too surprising, then, that many of these cases ended in acquittals, lower sentences than might seem warranted, or early paroles, due to the same vagaries of jurisprudence.

While we do revere our heroes, we can be quick to forget them. This is nothing new. Hal Gosling received a hero's funeral in February 1885. San Antonio delayed its Washington's Birthday celebration (in Gosling's era a holiday of patriotic import second only to Independence Day) to bury him with full honors. A scant year later, local papers lamented the sad, neglected state of his grave site. Six years after John Gilley's murder his hometown newspaper couldn't even get his name or the facts of his death correct.

May this book serve to keep alive the memory of those whose stories are told here. They, and all who serve, deserve our remembrance and respect. This sentiment is perhaps expressed by a more recent Kansas politician. At a dedication ceremony held at the State Law Enforcement Memorial in Topeka in May of 1997, Kansas attorney General Carla Stovall made the following statement. Its message is universal: "Let us never, never forget to honor law enforcement officers; those who have served and survived, those who have served and died, and those who serve us still."

Chapter 1: *"I've got more for the rest of you!"*
Police Officer Humphrey R. Symons
Gold Hill, Nevada (July 21, 1879)

He was an immigrant, born in the Breage parish of west Cornwall in 1844. As a young man Humphrey R. Symons had relocated to Gold Hill, Nevada. Spitting distance from Virginia City and smack in the heart of the Comstock Lode, Gold Hill was described as "the personification of a wild, young, rip-roaring frontier mining camp." "Cornish Jacks" settling in the States gravitated to mining regions. With skills forged in the copper and tin mines of their home country, they found ready work in the mines and stamp mills. Brutal, hazardous work, its main product was ore and its byproducts were widows and orphans. For a time, Symons worked the rich gold and silver mines, but he ended up on what likely seemed a safer career path; he became a police officer in Gold Hill.

One chronicler observed that "in Virginia City in its palmy days, there were no brakes on men and every boiler carried double pressure." It was an apt description of John T. Pritchard, a local ne'er-do-well and boozing blowhard. He shared a rough life, a rocky relationship, and a couple of rented rooms at the edge of town with Jennie Woodward, who called herself "Mrs. Pritchard."

On the evening of July 21, 1879, around 8:30 p.m., Pritchard and Woodward were at home, engaged in one of their customary screaming matches, which soon degenerated into a boxing match. Only one thing made this fight stand out from all the others: a pistol shot. The shot injured no one, but it sent the frantic landlady, Mrs. Casey, scurrying into the street to find help. She didn't have to go far.

Like most of his countrymen who had immigrated to the area, Humphrey Symons did the back-breaking job of a miner before he became a lawman. *(Photo courtesy of the Silver State National Peace Officers Museum)*

Humphrey Symons was walking up the street on the opposite side, possibly having heard the gunshot. Mrs. Casey breathlessly explained what was going on in Pritchard's quarters, and the policeman assured her he would take care of the matter.

Intervening in domestic disputes is one of a law enforcer's least favorite duties, and for good reason. Such incidents are emotionally charged – often aggravated by alcohol or drugs – and the parties doing battle will frequently and capriciously toss their differences aside and team up against anyone who dares meddle in their domestic chaos. The incidence of officers injured or killed handling domestic disputes is disproportionately high. Any modern peace officer knows this. Officers of any experience in Symons' time ought to have known it, too.

According to firsthand accounts (excepting Pritchard, who had obvious reasons for telling another tale), Symons strolled across the street and entered the Casey house in a casual way, his pipe in one hand and a cane in the other. He coolly informed Pritchard that he was under arrest for disturbing the peace. Pritchard's answer was immediate and to the point; he raised a bulldog revolver and fired.

Neighbors and passers-by heard two gunshots close together and another a few seconds later. Immediately, a small crowd gathered in the street outside the house. Pritchard stalked out onto the porch, full of bug juice as usual, and full of himself as always. He waved his pistol at the onlookers. He gloated that he'd just shot Symons and threatened the crowd, "I've got more for the rest of you!"

Gold Hill Marshal Folsom arrived at the scene shortly, accompanied by Constable Dan Donovan and at least one other officer. The obstreperous Pritchard had gone back inside, apparently satisfied he'd warned off any further meddling with his evening. While Donovan went around the back way, Folsom entered the house. He found Symons lying on the floor, bleeding profusely from ghastly head wounds. Pritchard was sitting on a nearby sofa. Mortally wounded but still alive, Symons just managed to gasp out, "Shoot him! Shoot him!" Folsom identified himself to Pritchard, whose answer was to spring from the sofa and pull his pistol from the pocket of his trousers. Folsom snapped a shot at him, hitting him in the right arm. A second shot misfired, so the marshal made a hasty tactical retreat onto the porch to reload, unsure whether he'd hit Pritchard. He arrested Woodward, who was still on the porch, then reentered the house. By this time Donovan had slipped in, gotten the drop on Pritchard, and disarmed and arrested him. Donovan handed over the revolver he'd taken from Pritchard; it held four expended cartridges and one live round.

Symons died shortly after. The officers found a fully loaded, five-shot English bulldog pistol still in his hip pocket. Bloody handprints all around the lawman's body showed that, wounded as he was, Symons had tried gamely to get to his feet. A post-mortem examination revealed three pistol wounds to the head. The first had entered just under his right eye and gone through his upper jaw; the second had entered the left cheek at the outer corner of the eye and skimmed along the base of his skull to just behind his left ear. The third shot struck about two and a half inches behind his right ear and drove a chunk of skull into his brain. Powder burns on Symons's face showed that the pistol had been quite close when fired. It appeared that Pritchard had shot him once, and shot again as he was falling or already down. Then as Symons struggled to stand, Pritchard – in what the *Gold Hill Evening News* would call "the malicious vindictiveness of his drunken soul," – had fired a coup de grâce into the back of his head.

Folsom lodged Pritchard in the jail at Virginia City, but only for the night. As the *Daily Nevada State Journal* reported, "Strong talk of lynching Pritchard, who so foully murdered officer Symons, is heard in Virginia. The sheriff is trying to prevent it." Symons was well-liked, and Storey County Sheriff Charles Williamson didn't want a lynching bee on his hands. He arranged to transfer Pritchard the following day to the state prison at Carson City, where he was held without bail pending his trial.

While in custody, Pritchard kept up his show of defiant bravado. He freely admitted shooting Symons, bragging that he'd shoot anyone who came into his house. If not for his own wound, Pritchard boasted, "I would have killed three or four more of the sons of bitches." While he dressed Pritchard's wound at the jail, county physician Dr. Kirby remarked (possibly hoping to elicit further incriminating statements) that rumors circulating through town claimed Pritchard hadn't shot

Symons. Pritchard angrily denounced such hogwash. He told the
doctor, "I shot the son of a bitch and don't deny it! If I hadn't been
shot myself, three or four others would have got it."

Later, presumably after some sober reflection, Pritchard shifted
from bluster to self-preservation in recounting the incident. His story
now was this: Symons had entered the house gun in hand, greeting
him with, "Good morning, Mr. Pritchard. You may consider yourself
under arrest." When Pritchard inquired as to the charge and whether
Symons had a warrant, Symons informed him the charge was
disturbing the peace, and that he would get his warrant when he
accompanied Symons to the city jail. Pritchard balked, and Symons
shot him in the arm. The rest, he claimed, was a matter of pure self
defense.

Early on, Pritchard was in danger of losing his arm from the
gunshot damage. Newspapers reported that doctors "found no sign of
knitting in the shattered bone. It may yet be necessary to open the arm
and wire the bone together. Even this may not save the bone."
Apparently, however, such predictions were premature. Pritchard kept
his arm.

Humphrey Symons, who'd died just ten days short of his thirty-
fifth birthday, was buried on July 23 in the Gold Hill Cemetery, under
an ornate marble headstone bearing the Odd Fellows seal. The *Gold
Hill Evening News* mourned him as "one of the best officers ever seen
in this section...slaughtered in the prime of his manhood." Symons
left behind a wife, Sarah, and five-year-old son, Henry. He was laid to
rest beside his daughter, Sarah, who had died two years earlier at age
eleven. Three other children of the couple rested nearby; each had
died in infancy. Sarah was carrying a sixth child at the time. A week
to the day after his father's death, Humphrey S. Symons was born.

At Pritchard's preliminary hearing on a charge of first degree
murder he was held to answer. Before his trial he asked for, and was
granted, a change of venue from Storey County to Ormsby County.

The trial was held at the beginning of December at the District Court in Carson City, Judge Samuel D. King presiding. "Colonel" Robert H. Taylor, a prominent Virginia City attorney, represented Pritchard. Even though the evidence was primarily circumstantial – i.e. no third party saw Pritchard kill Symons – the prosecution was confident of securing a conviction and a sentence of death.

Before the first witness even testified, the proceedings stalled with some heated wrangling over jury selection. After twelve jurors were examined came the defense's opportunity for peremptory challenges, whereby potential jurors could be rejected as unsuitable to try the case. Taylor passed. The prosecution, in its turn, issued several challenges and, "as often as a juror was challenged," court records state, "another name was drawn, thus keeping the panel full." One juror, Evan David, stated that since this was a death penalty case and the evidence circumstantial, he would not find Pritchard guilty. The prosecution challenged David for implied bias, and Judge King dismissed him. Throughout this process, Taylor passed several more opportunities to challenge jurors. Judge King advised him that in passing those challenges he would be deemed by the court to have accepted the jury as it stood. Taylor apparently accepted this admonition without protest. Then after – and only after – the state had concluded all its challenges, he suddenly insisted upon challenging one juror, C.O. Appleburg. Judge King denied the challenge, and Appleburg remained on the jury

After the legal tussling over the jury was through, the trial was a fairly straightforward affair lasting several days. Taylor stuck to Pritchard's claim that Symons, not Folsom, had shot him, and that he had acted in defense of his own life. The jury didn't buy it. On December 6 they deliberated a mere twenty minutes. The next day's *Daily Nevada State Journal* announced the result: "The trial of J.T. Pritchard, at Carson, for the murder of officer Symons, of Gold Hill, was concluded at 4 o'clock yesterday afternoon, the jury returning a verdict of murder in the first degree." Without a pica slug's space in between, the next line read, "Six inches of snow in Bodie." Perhaps this was evidence that the public was already moving on.

Judge King sentenced Pritchard to be hanged. His execution date was fixed at January 16, 1880. On December 18, the *Reno Evening Gazette* reported that the normally ebullient Pritchard was "sullen and somewhat reticent since his conviction." What a welcome relief this must have been to his jailers. The *Gazette* went on, "When he does speak, which is seldom, he talks senselessly about being persecuted and says he was sold even by his lawyer. This is the basest ingratitude, showing what an ungrateful creature the man is, for Col. Taylor made a good and ingenious defence [sic] of Pritchard. The fact is, Pritchard's killing of Symons was a dastardly murder, and his conviction surprised no one who had heard the testimony."

Base ingratitude or no, Taylor secured a delay in Pritchard's execution and a hearing before the Nevada Supreme Court to argue for a new trial. The hearing was scheduled for January 26, but was postponed due to the illness of Justice Thomas Hawley. The hearing commenced in early February with Attorney General Michael A. Murphy arguing for the state, and Taylor representing Pritchard. Over the next several days, Hawley and his fellow justices William Beatty and Chief Justice Orville Leonard listened intently to both sides. Taylor's argument was four-pronged. He maintained that (1) The court had erred in allowing juror David to be challenged and dismissed; (2) The court had erred in disallowing the defense's tardy challenge of juror Appleburg; (3) The court had given improper and insufficient instruction to the jury as to the distinctions between the various degrees of murder, manslaughter, and justifiable and excusable homicide; (4) The evidence presented at trial did not warrant a conviction for first degree murder.

On February 11, the Supreme Court adjourned, having heard all arguments in Pritchard's case but deferring their decision until after the court reconvened on March 1. On March 4 their decision came.

With regard to Taylor's first, third and fourth arguments, all three justices essentially agreed to uphold Judge King's actions and the jury's decision. As to the matter of juryman Appleburg, the justices were divided.

Hawley vigorously argued that whether defense attorneys had waived jury challenges "for an improper reason, or from motives of caprice," Judge King had acted properly in forcing them to stand by it. Beatty and Leonard did not agree. In their view, Judge King could have avoided the controversy altogether by swearing in the jurors one by one, as each passed all challenges, rather than as a group (both methods were allowed by Nevada law). By not doing so, Justice Beatty wrote, "...the right of the state to challenge any of the jurors in the box remained unaffected," – an obvious reference to juror David's dismissal – "while that of the defendant was effectively cut off."

As a result, the court reversed King's refusal to grant the defense motion for a new trial. John T. Pritchard was on his way back to court. The *Carson Tribune* reported that when this news reached Pritchard, "he was so overcome with joy that he could not speak." If Pritchard's reticence had delighted his keepers, his absolute silence must have sent them into fits of ecstasy.

Pritchard's new trial convened on July 20, 1880, nearly a year to the day after Symons' murder. Taylor again faced Judge King, assisted by a Carson City attorney, Nils Soderberg. William Woodburn argued for the state. At the first day's end, only two jurors from a pool of thirty had been chosen. Eighty prospective jurors were brought in the next day; the court was clearly taking no chances with jury selection this time around.

After the twelve jurors were sworn, Judge King – perhaps a bit gun shy over the Supreme Court's decision – allowed Soderberg to ask the jury en masse a pointed question. "Since you were examined by me before, touching your qualifications to serve as jurors," Soderberg asked the twelve, "has anything happened, or occurred, to your recollection, to render you improper jurors in this case to your knowledge?" As if on cue, juror J.C. Dorsey stood up and repeated nearly verbatim Evan David's statement from the first trial. Since this was a death penalty case and the evidence circumstantial, Dorsey explained, he would be reluctant to find Pritchard guilty. "I would hardly bring in a verdict of murder in the first degree unless it was very positive and personal evidence," he said.

Woodburn pounced. "Suppose there was no witness to the transaction," he pressed Dorsey, "no person who saw the defendant shoot Humphrey Symons (and) take his life, and his guilt depended upon circumstantial evidence, would you render such a verdict, a verdict in the first degree, when you knew the penalty was death?" Dorsey's answer was simple: "No sir, I would not."

Though the jurors had already been duly and properly sworn, Woodburn challenged Dorsey's qualifications based on implied bias. Under the circumstances Judge King allowed this ex post facto challenge. He excused Dorsey, overruling Soderberg's objection to his dismissal. Before another juror could be appointed in Dorsey's place, the defense moved that the remaining eleven be discharged and a new jury impaneled. When the court denied this motion, Soderberg moved for a new trial. Judge King denied this motion as well.

Once again, the legal drama over jury selection nearly eclipsed the actual trial. Newspaper coverage was more disinterested this time; the *Daily Nevada State Journal* could only grouse that, "The keeping and repeated trials of John T. Pritchard for the murder of officer Symons will cost the people of Storey County not less than $10,000."

Eight days in, the defense rested and the jury retired to deliberate. The following morning they announced their verdict. The *Reno Evening Gazette* reported jury votes "originally stood one for murder in the first degree, four for murder in the second degree, and seven for manslaughter." Per the *Gazette*, Judge King's instructions to the jury had been explicit: "If an officer having a warrant is resisted after giving proper notice of his authority and is slain, the offense is murder." He pointed out that if Symons had entered Pritchard's home to arrest him for a misdemeanor crime (disturbing the peace) not committed in Symons' presence, the attempted arrest was unlawful. "If Pritchard resisted an unlawful arrest," King went on, "and in the resistance killed Symonds [sic], the defendant can, at best, be found guilty of manslaughter." He wrapped up by informing the jury that there was no evidence Symons had seen Pritchard commit any offense before he entered Pritchard's home. Despite their initial division the jury seems, in the end, to have split the difference. They found Pritchard guilty of second degree murder.

Pritchard was convicted once again, but spared the noose. On August 5 Judge King sentenced him to life in the state penitentiary. Here, no doubt emboldened by his courtroom wins, Pritchard returned to his usual endearing behavior. Assigned to work in the prison stone quarry, he took on the task with what the newspapers called, "his natural disposition." After a few days, they said, Pritchard "refused to do another stroke of work, because he was tired. He is now confined in the dungeon for insubordinancy [sic]."

While Pritchard was kept busy making big rocks into small rocks – or refusing to – his attorneys busied themselves with a new round of appeals. Three months later, Pritchard's case again came before the Nevada Supreme Court. This time Justices Beatty, Leonard and Hawley heard from Soderberg, who argued that Judge King, by allowing the prosecution to challenge juror Dorsey after the jurors were sworn, by dismissing Dorsey from the jury, and by refusing to then dismiss the remainder of the jury, placed Pritchard in double jeopardy and thus denied him a fair trial.

This time around the justices were in total accord. In the unanimous opinion, Justice Hawley made clear whom the court held responsible for Dorsey's exclusion. "It must be remembered," he wrote, "that it was not the fault of the prosecution, nor of the court, that the incompetency of the juror was not discovered until after the jury was sworn, and that the knowledge of the juror's incompetency was brought out by the voluntary act of defendant's counsel." If King erred at all, the justices held, it was in allowing Soderberg to ask the jury his question at all. "Counsel should not, in our opinion," Hawley wrote, "have been allowed to fish out of season for some point on which to lay a foundation for an exception, without, at least, first baiting his hook in a proper manner." The short answer was: "The judgment of the district court is affirmed." Pritchard's conviction stood.

Pritchard remained a ward of the state. Back when he was facing the gallows he had written to Jennie Woodward, asking her to come and visit him in prison, but there is no evidence that she did, then or ever. In July 1891, Pritchard's application for parole was summarily denied.

The Nevada State Prison housed John Pritchard after the Nevada Supreme Court spared him from the hangman's noose. *(Author's Collection)*

Sarah Symons, meanwhile, remained in Gold Hill and Virginia City. She worked as a dressmaker and raised her two boys, Henry and Humphrey. The younger Symons remained in Gold Hill all his life.

He worked as a teamster and a miner, owned mining properties, and became something of a local mover and shaker. He served as a member of the school board, on the county central committee, and as a fireman in Gold Hill's historic Liberty Engine Company No. 1.

Sarah Symons died in Gold Hill on October 11, 1924, having never remarried. Both her sons were at her side when she died. Her obituary mentioned she was "the widow of Humphrey Symons, once a police officer of Virginia City [sic] who was killed in line of duty 45 years ago." In September 1951, Humphrey S. Symons died in bed at his home in Gold Hill. He was seventy-two years old. A couple of cousins in California were the only family he had left. His obituary briefly mentioned Humphrey's father, the brave Gold Hill lawman of so long ago.

A line in the obituaries of the wife who outlived him by forty–five years and of a son who never knew him was about the most tribute paid Humphrey Symons for his sacrifice in the century after his death. In 2003, the Nevada Law Enforcement Officers Memorial added his name to its monument after Frank Adams, a retired Nevada Department of Public Safety investigator, and Steve Frady, a former firefighter, came across old newspaper accounts of his killing. Visitors to the state capitol grounds at Carson City can see Symons' name there today.

He is the first Nevada lawman known to have been killed while responding to a domestic dispute. It's a dubious distinction. But Humphrey Symons worked in a rough, untamed town in a period when a lawman often had no one to rely on but himself. In giving up one brutally tough line of work for another and trying to bring order to the place he called home, he gave his all. If he is remembered, it ought to be for that. What's most important, though, is that he be remembered.

This photo of Gold Hill was taken a dozen or so years before Humphrey Symons policed its sprawling streets. *(Photo courtesy of the National Archive and Records Administration)*

Chapter 2: *"Hollister was one of the bravest and most daring men on the border, and was a terror to evil doers."*
Deputy Sheriff Cassius M. Hollister
Sumner County, Kansas (October 18, 1884)

Caldwell's luck with lawmen had not been good. If they weren't being killed in private quarrels or shooting at one another, they had a tendency to switch sides and go on the owlhoot trail. Cash Hollister, it seemed, was just what the town – and later the county and federal court district – needed. Born December 7, 1845, (though his gravestone says July 7) near Cleveland, Ohio, Cassius M. Hollister came to Kansas at the age of 31. On July 29, 1878, he married Sarah "Sadie" Rhodes in Caldwell, and the couple lived briefly in Wichita before returning to Caldwell and the borderlands. Hollister took a job as clerk of the St James Hotel, where he worked until October of 1879. By that time Cash was a father; his daughter, Wilda "Wildie" Hollister (mistakenly listed as "son" in the 1880 census), was born in August of 1879.

In late September Caldwell's mayor, Noah Dixon, died suddenly. A special election was held a month later to fill the vacancy, and local interests persuaded Hollister to run for the seat. On October 20 the *Caldwell Post* announced the results: "C.M. Hollister was elected Mayor by a majority of eleven, on Tuesday last, over his opponent, W. N. Hubbell. The contest was close and everything went off smoothly, with a general good feeling among the candidates and people in general." As contentious as Caldwell politics could be, this said much for Hollister's reputation about town.

Not a month after taking office, the new mayor was arrested by his own City Marshal, George Flatt, for assault on Frank Hunt. He was fined $1.00 and costs in police court on November 22. Two days later Hunt was similarly fined for assaulting Hollister. During his tenure as mayor, Hollister's name would crop up now and again in the court's docket for a variety of minor violations. Although the local papers reported that Mayor Hollister served "faithfully and well," when the regular city election was held in the spring of 1880 he declined to run. He was replaced in early April by Mike Meagher. Frank Hunt would serve on the city's police force during Meagher's tenure.

The former mayor and new father seems to have found public service to his liking; he served variously as City Marshal, Deputy Marshal, and Special Policeman. Now his name frequently appeared on the other side of the police court dockets. As the local newspapers would later describe his law enforcement career, Hollister was "always one of the first called upon to make arrests of bad men and was very successful in this line of business."

In early 1883, Benjamin Franklin Simpson, U.S. Marshal for the Kansas District, commissioned Hollister a Deputy U.S. Marshal. Such multiple commissions were common among lawmen of the day, as it broadened their jurisdictional authority considerably. A year later Hollister would also be appointed a Sumner County Deputy Sheriff. The federal commission, especially, would have been a boon to a local officer working so near the border of the Indian Territory, particular along the infamous Cherokee Strip.

One of the newly-minted federal deputy's first official acts was aiding in the pursuit and capture of a horse thief. On March 18, 1883, a "Captain Nipp" and "Mr. McIntyre" arrived from Arkansas City on the trail of one Frank Hostetter. The three lawmen found their man across the border near Johnson's Ranch, in the company of a confederate named Jay Wilkinson. The latter made his escape on a horse stolen from Johnson, while Hostetter was arrested and returned to Arkansas City to face trial before the federal court. Horse theft was serious business, especially in the treacherous border territory, where being left afoot was tantamount to a death sentence. The *Caldwell Commercial* expressed the local sentiment towards such acts with a caveat: "If the thieves don't have a care, some of them may find themselves at the end of a rope one of these fine spring mornings."

The following month Deputy U.S. Marshal Hollister would again trail horse thieves, this time from the Lone Star state. A fellow named Herron came up from Clay County, Texas, on the trail of a band of thieves who had relieved him of two horses, two mules and various other livestock. He and Hollister set out after the group, and "run foul" of the party a few miles southeast of Hunnewell, Kansas. The ragtag family band consisted of Sam Ross, his wife, his daughter, two sons and the wife and child of one of the sons. Hollister suspected another small party camped nearby of being in cahoots with the Ross group and, seeing the numbers against him and Herron, backtracked into Caldwell to enlist the aid of City Marshal Henry Brown and his deputy, Ben Wheeler. Like the fabled Three Guardsman of the Indian Territory, Hollister, Brown and Wheeler would over the next year share a number of adventures, to the dismay of many a bad man along the border.

Returning to the Ross camp, the three men stopped briefly in Hunnewell and sought out additional support – City Marshal Jackson and Sumner County Deputy Sheriff Wes Thralls. The intrepid posse made straight for the Ross camp and per the *Caldwell Commercial*, "At grey dawn, surrounded the outfit." Answering a call for surrender, the Rosses "opened fire with their Winchesters." The lawmen followed suit, and a hot battle continued for the next half hour, during which Sam Ross and elder son James both fell dead, and the younger Ross son was badly wounded "in two or three places." Left alone to face the consequences, young Ross admitted the group had left Texas with "about forty head of horses and mules, among their number, a fine stallion, for which a reward for $500 is offered." They had apparently sold off most of the stock in Wichita.

In late May, Hollister, Brown and Wheeler made a less flamboyant arrest when they corralled a young drifter names John

Caypless who had stolen a saddle from a Caldwell livery stable. After getting a confession from their man, the officers took him to the spot, several miles from town, where he claimed his "partners" (who were conveniently absent) had stored the rig. The *Caldwell Journal* reported that Hollister and his colleagues "taking into consideration that he had packed the saddle to its hiding place, concluded that he could carry it back to town, which he did."

In early August, Hollister arrested another stock thief, this time without bloodshed. He had received a notice to be on the lookout for John Moore, who had taken a span of mules from the Cheyenne and Arapaho agency. Hollister spotted his man "coming up with the Indian train last week," said the *Journal*, and Moore "dropped into Hollister's hands like a ripe apple."

Cash Hollister's next big outing as a federal officer was a corker. The *Caldwell Journal* proclaimed:

PROBABLE MURDER
A Man and Woman Arrested

The lurid headline was only a hint at what would prove to be a sensational and high-profile case. In early October, Hollister was notified of a killing that had occurred on Hackberry Creek, near Skeleton Ranch in the Indian Territory (about a mile south of present day Enid, Oklahoma). A party traveling from Newton, Kansas, bound with a herd of sheep for Texas, had stopped for the night. The group consisted of an Englishman, Clement Bothamley, his "sister" Nellie C. Bailey, and two hired men, William Dodson and Wesley Vetter. On the night of October 18, a distraught Nellie Bailey had summoned Dodson to the wagon she shared with Bothamley. When Dodson entered the vehicle, a covered sheepwagon converted into a sort of early camper, he found Bothamley lying on the couple's makeshift bed, dead of a gunshot wound to the head. Bailey's story, which would fluctuate wildly throughout the subsequent inquiries, was that

Bothamley had committed suicide. Where she was and what she was doing when this happened varied from telling to telling. The group took Bothamley's body to Skeleton Ranch where they buried it in a box made from old storage crates, and Dodson set out for Caldwell to report the death. The incident having occurred on federal land, Cash Hollister rode out to the scene, once more taking along Henry Brown and Ben Wheeler. Bailey and the two herders had by then continued on their way; Hollister and the Caldwell officers caught up with them about nine miles south of Skeleton Ranch.

Hollister arrested Bailey, Dodson and Vetter, and the party returned to Caldwell. Meanwhile, A.W. Carr, a representative of the British Association of Kansas, had been notified of Bothamley's death and requested that his countryman's body be exhumed. Hollister returned to Skeleton Ranch with a zinc casket and brought back Bothamley's remains. After an examination in Caldwell, which ruled out suicide, Bothamley's body was returned to Newton for proper burial.

When arrested, Bailey was in possession of "a lot of diamond jewelry" and "about 300 pounds of silverware" determined to belong to Bothamley. Hollister confiscated this property, valued at about $7,000, and turned it over to the court, along with 2200 head of sheep. There was also the matter of Bothamley's ranch property in Sedgwick County, which he had deeded just prior to leaving Kansas to "Sarah Laws" – who proved to be Nellie Bailey.

A hearing in the Bailey case was held in late October before the U.S. District Court in Wichita. Both Vetter and Dodson testified, along with a man named Collins from Skeleton Ranch. Collins said Bailey had told him she was Bothamley's sister, and that they were both from England. She also told him they had at one point left Bothamley behind in Kansas due to illness, but had returned for him.

Dodson testified that he had found Bothamley lying on the floor of the wagon with his head toward the rear door and a bullet hole under his right eye, with a wound at the back of the head. He said that at Skeleton Ranch he had washed and "laid out" Bothamley's body for burial.

Bailey's case seemed damaged when details of her prior marriages (one in 1879 to Shannon Bailey, and a later one – while still Mrs. Bailey – to Robert Riese) came out. No charges were brought against Dodson and Vetter, but Bailey was indicted and held over. "Owing, we suppose, to the sympathetic efforts of several soft-hearted females in Wichita," groused the *Caldwell Journal*, her bail was set at $10,000. No matter – she was unable to make bail and remained in jail until her trial. For reasons utterly unrelated to her case, none of the three Kansas officers who arrested Nellie Bailey would live to see her acquitted on January 19, 1885. Brown and Wheeler died in May 1884, after a botched bank holdup in which they were not the lawmen, but the robbers. At least they were spared the indignity of being libeled in a pair of self-serving, nearly identical books Nellie co-wrote (or ghost-wrote), which portrayed her as the model of Victorian virtue and innocence and the officers as corrupt and brutish – ideal villains for her little melodrama.

She took the books on the lecture circuit in her own period version of a modern reality show. "Nellie C. Bailey has been in the city this week canvassing for her book," reported the *Arkansas City Traveler* in November. It declared that said book "though written in the form of a romance, is by no means a fiction; the material which composes it is mostly based on sworn testimony."

And so it was – defense testimony; very little of the prosecution's case found its way onto Nellie's purple pages. "We have not the space to devote to review of the book," the *Traveler* went on, "but it is an interesting volume. It is truly a Kansas book." Whatever that meant.

One of Cash Hollister's most notable arrests was that of Nellie Bailey – whom he would not live to see acquitted for murder. *(Author's Collection)*

The Bailey case, while definitely the most lurid and headline grabbing, was neither Hollister's last nor his most exciting exploit.

Scarcely a month after he had collared Nellie, his latest arrest made its own dramatic headline in the *Caldwell Journal*:

A MAN FOR SUPPER
Killed Because He Would Not Surrender

The man in question was Chester Van Meter, a twenty-something hardcase who lived with his wife and father-in-law on a small farm about nine miles from Caldwell. Described by a local newspaper as "one of the blood and thunder kind of young men," Van Meter had been in jail a year earlier for a scrape in which he'd shot at the Cowley County Sheriff, and during that stretch had been caught more than once attempting to break jail.

Time behind bars apparently taught Van Meter nothing. The evening of November 20, 1883, he'd gone on a spree. He had beaten his wife and father-in-law and shot at a couple of citizens, J.W. Loverton and "Miss Dotie." For good measure, the next morning he also pummeled his teenage brother-in-law, then made it known that he "would kill half a dozen of them in that neighborhood before he got through." Cash Hollister was detailed to bring Van Meter in. He took Ben Wheeler along, and the two found Van Meter at his father's place, a dozen or so miles from town. The young ruffian stood at the corner of the house brandishing a Winchester when they rolled up. The lawmen jumped from their wagon and ordered Van Meter to raise his hands, but he elected to take a pot shot at Hollister instead. Hollister and Wheeler returned fire without effect. As Van Meter raised his rifle to shoot again, the officers loosed another salvo and dropped him in the dust. They hauled his body back to Caldwell, where a coroner's jury, convened that same afternoon, found the killing justified. "All such men end the same way," said the *Winfield Courier*, without sympathy, "(they) beat their wives and die with their boots on." The *Caldwell Journal* was more hopeful: "And thus the latest, and we trust the last, sensation [sic] incident to border life in Kansas has ended."

But neither the Kansas border towns nor Cash Hollister were destined to be that lucky. In February 1884, Hollister was appointed a deputy sheriff by Sumner County Sheriff Frank Henderson. His last outing while still a federal deputy seems to have been the September 1884 arrest for violation of state prohibition laws of Frank Swarz, who operated a rowdy dance hall about twelve miles west of Caldwell. The place had been operating nearly non-stop, including Sundays, and was so disreputable that Hollister and his fellow lawmen were concerned "that if a stop was not put to it, someone would be killed in a drunken brawl, and Caldwell be blamed for it."

A week later, on September 11, the *Caldwell Journal* reported that Cash Hollister had resigned his position as Deputy U.S. Marshal. The issue, it appears, was not Cash but *cash*; like many a federal deputy before and after him, Hollister seems to have had difficulty in getting Uncle Sam to pay up. "The marshal and others connected with the office," the paper said, "appear to want Cash to do the work, and then not have any of the pay for the same, which, of course, he kicks about. There ought to be a deputy marshal here," the *Journal* complained of the government's oversights, "… but there seems to be a feeling extant that the thing must not be allowed."

Scarcely a month later, Deputy Sheriff Hollister was hunting a man who had run off with the proverbial farmer's daughter. But this was no joke. Robert Cross, a Texas transplant who'd come up with a herd in the spring of 1883, had promptly sold a borrowed horse and been a nuisance to citizens, lawmen and judges in the border region ever since, had finally gone too far. On October 12, Cross, married with child, had stolen away with the teenage daughter of local farmer Joshua Hannum, taking her to Cedar Vale in Chautauqua County. After four days together, the pair traveled back to Wellington, where Cross put the girl – presumably no longer a blushing maiden – on a Caldwell-bound train with a promise to meet her the following day. As the naïve girl rode home alone, Cross met his wife in Bluff Township, near Caldwell, and they went to the home of his brother-in-law, Fin Warrensburg, near Hunnewell. Cross and Warrensburg were already in dutch for vandalism and assault committed at a "Jew store" on the county line, so the fact that Cross chose to lie low at his known cohort's home says much about his mental acuity.

When the trusting Miss Hannum arrived safely in Caldwell and found no trace of her Texas two-timer, she did what most young girls in similar straits did – ran home to daddy. Her father promptly went into Caldwell and swore out a warrant for Cross's arrest. This warrant, along with two others for the "Jew store" incident, was given to Cash Hollister for service. Along with Hannum and Deputy George Davis, Cash set out in a wagon after his man on the evening of October 17, 1884. Having suspicion that Cross was holed up at Warrensburg's house, Cash stopped in Hunnewell and enlisted the aid of a town marshal named Riley (also reported as Reilly). The party headed from there to the Warrensburg house, about a mile north and two miles west of Hunnewell. They arrived about 3 a.m. the following day.

Leaving Hannum in charge of the team, Hollister and the other lawmen approached the house and shouted for Cross to surrender. They were answered from within by Mrs. Cross and another woman – probably Mrs. Warrensburg – who denied that Cross was in the house. One of the men kicked open the door and the two women came out and "swore by all they held sacred" – not much it would appear – that Cross was not home. Duly skeptical, Hollister insisted that the women light a lamp so he could see inside the house. They refused, instead retreating inside and slamming the door. Again the door was kicked open. This time the response from within was more pointed. Two gunshots narrowly missed the officers standing silhouetted in the doorway.

"The officers became more cautious," was the *Caldwell Journal*'s understatement. The men took better tactical positions – Hollister at the southwest corner of the house, guarding the door; Davis at another corner in sight of him; Riley opposite Hollister at the northeast corner, keeping watch on two windows. Hollister shouted a final warning to the women: unless Cross showed himself, the lawmen would burn the house.

The women came out, still claiming to be alone, and begged the lawmen to desist. Ignoring their pleas, Davis fetched hay and began packing it under the house. Another shot came from inside and Hollister dropped – to avoid further gunfire, Davis thought at first. He took cover behind a large wood pile, and when he sneaked a look around it and saw that Hollister hadn't moved, Davis feared the worst. Risking a break from his makeshift fortress, he scurried to Hollister's side and saw that he'd been shot and appeared to be dead.

Davis shouted to Riley that Hollister was down. The city marshal shouted back for Davis to guard the door but, as the *Caldwell Journal* put it, "Davis' only thought then was to get Hollister away." As Riley came around to cover the door Davis picked up Hollister's body and carried it to the wagon. As he tried to load Hollister aboard, the team spooked, broke away from Hannum, and ran. With some difficulty, Davis and Hannum caught the rig, calmed the horses down and returned to where Hollister lay. They placed him into the wagon bed, and Davis returned to assist Riley.

In the confusion following Hollister's shooting, Mrs. Cross had slipped back into the house. As Riley was moving to cover the door, she reemerged, followed by her husband. Bob was barefoot, wearing only a shirt, and carrying a Winchester rifle and a pistol. The pair sidled along the front of the house, Cross following closely behind his wife, careful to keep her between him and danger. As they passed the corner of the house, Riley threw down on Cross with his own Winchester. The quick-thinking and overly-loyal Mrs. Cross "sprang between the men, grasped the gun, placed the muzzle to her breast and held it there." That was Cross's cue; he took to his heels. Riley wrenched his rifle free and leveled off for a shot at the fleeing man, but again Mrs. Cross grabbed the muzzle and held it to her body, until Bob had vanished into the gloom.

Riley was forced to settle for arresting the two women. He marched them to the wagon and the entire group, with Cash Hollister's body aboard, drove back into Hunnewell. Riley telephoned Mayor Morris of Caldwell and informed him of Hollister's death. After securing a fresh team of horses, Riley and Davis struck out for Caldwell with their prisoners and their tragic cargo. Meanwhile, a party had ridden out from Caldwell to meet them. The entire group arrived back in Caldwell about 10:30 a.m. Riley immediately set out again on Cross's trail with a posse led by Caldwell's assistant marshal, Bedford Wood.

News of Hollister's killing went out immediately, and lawmen and volunteers from neighboring towns and counties soon joined in the hunt for Bob Cross. "A large party are in pursuit of him," reported the *Lawrence Journal World*, "and if he is caught, he will be hanged to the first object that will support his weight." Luckily for Cross, trees were scarce along the Kansas/Indian Territory border. Meanwhile, he had stolen a pair of overalls, and around the time the Davis and Riley party rolled into Caldwell, Cross had crossed into the Indian Territory. Shortly after entering the Territory, he encountered an old man with a horse. Cross relieved the man of his mount "by the persuasive power of a Winchester rifle," and rode for the Chikaskia River. Near the banks of the river Cross's progress was halted by a barbed wire fence. He abandoned his stolen mount and began picking his way on foot up the river bed. The soft sand was a plus – Cross still wore no boots – and he followed the bed about two miles upstream then made his way to Bluff Creek. Several hundred yards from the river, he found rest and concealment in a small ravine.

The Wood and Riley group knew that Cross, afoot and shoeless, would find the going slow. It made sense that he would head for the Indian Territory, so they kicked for the border. They immediately encountered Cross's elderly robbery victim and learned that the fugitive had obtained a horse. The posse "struck Cross's trail where he had left his horse and followed it until he reached Bluff Creek where it was lost." They knew he couldn't have gone much further so they fanned out and "searched every bunch of grass, ravine, brush pile or hollow," and at around 4 p.m. – less than twelve hours after he had killed Cash Hollister – "they finally discovered him lying flat on the ground in a little draw." When he saw he'd been spotted, Cross made a feint for his rifle. "Two shots," reported the *Caldwell Journal*, "were fired in close proximity to his person to intimidate him and his capture was at once and easily effected."

Cross was still carrying the rifle he had used to kill Hollister. Without his wife to shield him now, he meekly surrendered it to Marshal Riley. When the officers informed him that he'd killed Hollister, leaving the lawman's wife and child without support, Cross callously remarked that he had a wife and child himself. He readily admitted the killing, stating that he had thought that if he "could get him (Hollister) out of the way, he could get away from the other fellows."

Word of the murderer's capture quickly spread through the region, as did talk of lynching. The *Dodge City Times* reported, "Bob Cross, the murderer of Deputy Sheriff Hollister, of Hunnewell [sic], was captured by officers who passed through here with the prisoner. They are endeavoring to evade a mob of two hundred men, who were in close pursuit, being at one time within six miles of the officers and their prisoner."

The posse took Cross to Hunnewell, then transferred him under close guard to the county jail at Wellington about 10 p.m. The *Caldwell Journal* observed "it is well they started when they did, or his body would have been found hanging to a telegraph pole the next morning."

Meanwhile, County Coroner R.W. Stephensen came from Wellington to Caldwell and conducted an inquest which lasted from October 18 to the evening of the 20th. The evidence was clear, despite Mrs. Cross' transparent attempts to shield her husband. She swore that not only had he not been present at the time of Hollister's shooting, but that there had been no men nor firearms whatsoever in the house. Her testimony "was taken with a large grain of allowance" – more than it merited – and the jury's verdict was that Cross had killed Hollister "with what is commonly known as a Winchester rifle loaded with gunpowder and leaden bullets and that the killing was felonious."

Upon his conviction for manslaughter in the killing of Cash Hollister, Bob Cross became prisoner #3453 in the Kansas State Penitentiary at Lansing. (*Author's Collection*)

Hollister was buried in the Caldwell City Cemetery at 10 a.m. on October 19, leaving behind his 22-year-old wife and five-year-old child. Nearly the entire city of Caldwell turned out to pay respects and per the *Journal*, "the moans of his widow at the last parting of the grave were enough to chill the heart of stone." While the widow grieved, others swore under their breath that Cross would suffer swift retribution if the law "failed to reward him with iron bars or the hangman's noose."

The *Wichita Daily Eagle* eulogized Hollister as "a brave officer and a true man." The *Lawrence Journal World* summed up his character and career thus: "Hollister was one of the bravest and most daring men on the border and was a terror to evildoers."

On January 5, 1885, Cross was convicted of manslaughter in the first degree for Hollister's killing. He was shipped off to the state prison at Lansing, where he began serving a fifteen-year term.

On March 1, 1893, the *Daily Eagle* reported that Hollister's wife had "made the run into Oklahoma and earned her claim, but unfortunately some parties are giving her trouble with a contest, although she has beaten them repeatedly." Mrs. Hollister had friends, the paper said, "numbered by the thousands, all of whom are hoping that she will be able to keep her land." Apparently she did. "Mrs. Hollister," reported the *Wichita Daily Eagle* later, "a most estimable lady now owns a fine farm in Hennessey (Oklahoma Territory), but she lives most of the time in this city, where she is regarded very highly by the physicians as a private nurse for the sick." She was still reported living on the farm three years later when Cross was released from prison.

In December 1896, Kansas Governor Edmund Morrill, a lame duck who had just been defeated for a second term, pardoned Cross and restored his full rights of citizenship.

The death of Cash Hollister in 1884 brought an abrupt end to the career of a lawman who, had he lived and continued to work as a peace officer, would likely be as well-remembered today as any of the celebrated legends of the wild old days.

The dusty streets of Caldwell are congested with wagon traffic as Kansans prepare to make the first Oklahoma land run, nearly five years after Cash Hollister's death. *(Photo courtesy of the Kansas State Historical Board)*

**Chapter 3: *"Well, I didn't believe they would try it."*
United States Marshal Hal Gosling
Western District, Texas (February 21, 1885)**

"How they peppered us! I am full of holes," Jim Pitts complained, as he and Charlie Yeager leaped from the International and Great Northern Express train near the Guadalupe River bridge just north of New Braunfels, Texas. It was true enough; varying accounts place between two and seven lead slugs in Pitts' body (the smart money's on four) as he and Yeager hit the ground and began running. The words would be his last. The pair made it only about ninety feet before Pitts sank to the ground. Yeager dragged him a few yards further and then eased down beside his dying partner. He had no choice; heavy steel manacles linked their wrists together. Though Yeager had always looked up to his older partner, his survival instinct quickly displaced hero worship. His only concern now was how to get free of his fix. As he pondered the situation he spied a large, sharp-edged rock – not so heavy it could shatter steel links, but plenty enough to bash through meat, cartilage and bone…

It's tough to feel sorry for Jim Pitts. He was a fleeing a rightful prison sentence and had left several dead or – for all he knew or cared – dying people aboard the train, at least one of whom he'd personally shot. A string of bad choices made of his own free will had led him to this place. And he'd likely have breathed a few years longer – albeit the rank air of a prison cell – had he not chosen to take mean advantage of the kindly nature of the lawman charged with ferrying him and Yeager to the pen.

Harrington Lee Gosling wasn't a career peace officer. The Tennessee native and Annapolis graduate was an attorney and journalist – editor/publisher of *The Castroville* (Texas) *Quill* – when his active participation in Republican politics garnered him an 1882 appointment as United States Marshal for the Western District of Texas. A genial sort by all accounts, he was described by one as, "a big, bluff, kindly, rollicking daredevil, afraid of nothing." Whether his kind nature, his fearlessness, or both, were to blame, Hal Gosling's errors in judgment on February 21, 1885, cost three lives. One was his own.

Former lawyer and journalist Harrington Lee Gosling was a newspaper editor when President Chester Arthur appointed him U.S. Marshal for the Western District of Texas. *(Photo courtesy of the Texas Press Association)*

James B. Pitts (also known as Tom Pitts and Jim Hall/Hale) and Charles Yeager, on the other hand, were nobody's idea of kindly. Known desperadoes, they ran with a confederation of miscreants known variously as the "Robbers' Cave Gang" or the "Helotes Gang." Robbing and murdering thugs, whom the newspapers described as "young in years but old in crime," the gang tore a bloody swath across south Texas throughout the early 1880s. Pitts was reputed to be a cousin of Charlie Pitts, who'd ridden with Jesse and Frank James and died in their gang's disastrous 1876 bank robbery attempt at Northfield, Minnesota. A 30-ish career criminal who'd done state prison time alongside John Wesley Hardin, Jim Pitts was known as "an old road agent, train robber, and murderer, and a man of undoubted nerve." At 23, Charlie Yeager was an eager accomplice – described by a fellow outlaw as "Pitts' tool, the lesser villain in every way."

One of the Helotes Gang's recent capers, the robbery of a post office at Smithwick in Burnett County – about seventy miles from Austin – had landed Pitts and Yeager in Austin's federal court. There, on the morning of February 21st, they were convicted of robbery and sentenced to ninety-nine years each. Upon the gavel's fall, Judge E.B. Turner charged Marshal Gosling with escorting Pitts and Yeager from Austin to the San Antonio jail, thence to the federal penitentiary at Chester, Illinois. Gosling chose Deputy U.S. Marshals John Manning and Fred Loring to accompany him. Manning was an experienced hand – a short, thick-necked, no-nonsense lawman described as "sober, gentlemanly, reliable," yet a man who "would rather fight than eat." Loring had experience not only as a deputy, but as a train conductor – knowledge that would prove handy before this assignment was over.

During the trial several of the defendants' female relatives, in court to testify on their behalf, had been allowed to sit just behind

The federal courthouse in Austin was the site of Jim Pitts' and Charles Yeager's robbery trial. *(Photo courtesy of the Austin History Center, Austin Public Library)*

them at the railing. Throughout the proceedings, Melissa – Pitts' wife of four months – her sister Annie Scott, his grandmother Elizabeth Drown, and Yeager's sister, Rosa Yeager, freely conversed in whispers with the two men. Mrs. Drown was a bulky matron of about 60 years, whose home was reputed to be a hideout for the Helotes Gang – a supposition bolstered by the 1880 Bexar County census, which listed her occupation as "rents her farm." Annie Scott and Rosa Yeager were young ladies still in their teens; Melissa Pitts was only slightly older.

After the sentence was pronounced, Manning handcuffed Pitts and Yeager together and walked them into the grand jury room. They were under guard, so the women were permitted to wait with them while Gosling made transportation arrangements. Here, more murmured communications took place. One of Gosling's other deputies, Gordon Walker, warned the marshal that he feared the group was cooking up an escape attempt. The defendants' own lawyer, M.G. "Mac" Anderson, expressed similar suspicions to Judge Turner, mainly out of concern "that no part in the performance should be attributed to him." Gosling paid these cautions little heed other than to have Walker and another deputy, Farris, accompany his group to the railroad depot, where they would board the late train for San Antonio. On the way, they stopped at Salge's chop house and Gosling, a gentleman from the ground up, treated the two prisoners to "a costly dinner."

Manning, meanwhile, had observed the whispered courtroom conferences and noted the presence in court of many more of the defendants' relations and friends, including several of their hard case pals. His keen law dog sense smelled trouble. He asked Gosling if anyone knew their itinerary, and Gosling admitted he'd told Carroll Brannon that they'd be going by the afternoon train. Carroll's brothers Joe and Dick were among the worst of the Helotes bunch; Dick Brannon was currently standing trial for his part in the Smithwick post office robbery, and Joe was in Missouri recovering from a shooting scrape in which he'd been – like Mark Twain – prematurely reported dead.

When Manning heard this, and learned that many of these folks – Carroll Brannon among them – planned to board the same train, he urged Gosling to postpone the trip until the next day. Gosling waved this off as he had the earlier warnings. To Manning's horror, the marshal even ordered him to unshackle the prisoners in the restaurant, that they might eat their meal in comfort. After lunch, as Manning prepared to cuff the prisoners together again, Pitts presented his left hand and Yeager his right. Manning balked – they'd had the opposite wrists connected earlier – but Pitts pleaded a sore wrist, so Manning grudgingly complied.

At the depot, the lawmen found the Pitts and Yeager contingent ready to board. Melissa Pitts tearfully begged Gosling's permission to ride to San Antonio alongside her husband. Here, chivalry and compassion completely got the better of Gosling's common sense. He agreed to allow the ladies in the party, along with several of the men, to share the smoking car that would carry him, Manning, Loring, and their prisoners.

Gosling bid Deputies Walker and Farris goodbye, and the motley group climbed aboard. Near the rear of the smoker, a pair of bench seats on either side of the aisle had been turned facing each other. On the right side, the marshals seated Pitts and Yeager against the wall facing one another, their manacled arms reaching across the space between the benches. Mrs. Pitts sat beside her husband and Rosa Yeager next to her brother.

Across the aisle from the prisoners, Gosling and Loring took the facing aisle seats and Manning took the window seat next to Loring. Will Lambert, a friend of Gosling's and a former newspaperman himself, happened to be aboard. A former Chief Clerk of the state legislature, Lambert was returning from business in Austin. At Gosling's invitation, he took the window seat beside the marshal.

Thomas Jefferson Scott, father of Melissa Pitts and Annie Scott, sat just ahead of the Yeagers. Beyond him sat the other assorted Pitts-Yeager followers, with Carroll Brannon several rows ahead in the car's front row.

As they were boarding, "Grandmother" Drown indicated the seat just behind Pitts and pleaded with Gosling, "Mayn't I sit here by Tom? It seems I am going to his funeral, and I have so much to say to him about Annie." Gosling assented and, Lambert later recalled, even "assisted the old vixen" to her requested place, seating Annie Scott beside her on the aisle.

Will Lambert was a fellow journalist and friend of Gosling's, and a witness to the daring escape that claimed the marshal's life. *(Author's Collection)*

Gosling, at least, found the seating arrangement tactically sound. He was facing Yeager on the oblique, and could view the others of the party beyond, all the way to Brannon. His deputies likewise faced Pitts. Thus, both prisoners were in view, and any danger could be easily foreseen. Or so he thought.

The train pulled out about 4:30 p.m. All went smoothly for the first hour and a half of the journey. The Pitts' whispered conference behind a newspaper seemed to raise no particular concern. Melissa Pitts and Rosa Yeager cried much of the way and hung about the necks of the prisoners. This seemed natural; Pitts and his wife were still newlyweds, and the men were going away for a very long time, likely for good. As the train came within five or six miles of New Braunfels, just past the halfway point between Austin and San Antonio, Melissa Pitts and Rosa Yeager abruptly repaired to the adjoining ladies' car carrying with them a small black valise. Lambert and Loring were watching. Though he later recalled thinking that "there was death in that grip," Lambert expressed no suspicion to his companions. When the two women returned several minutes later they were without their piece of luggage and, according to Lambert, their demeanor was "sad, as though going to a funeral."

If Gosling or the others found any of this behavior worrisome, it didn't show. Though he'd stepped out on the platform at every stop to see, according to Lambert's later statements, "that no allies of the prisoners were at the station to aid any attempt at rescue," the marshal appeared at ease with the known cohorts inside the smoking car. In Lambert's view Gosling treated his prisoners "more like friends than a brace of the most villainous desperadoes ever consigned to the keeping of an officer." To the ladies he showed "a manner becoming a Chesterfield." From a modern perspective, it's difficult to comprehend this. Though his peace officer experience was limited, Gosling was a lawyer and a newspaperman. Folks in those vocations were lied to as often as lawmen were. It just wasn't within the average Victorian gentleman's thinking, even that of a seasoned fellow like John Manning, to suspect treachery on the part of the fairer sex. Perhaps the ladies' presence put the lawmen more at ease with the men as well. In any case, while Gosling and his deputies focused some vigilance on the men, they paid scant attention to the women. Unfortunately for them, this seems to be just what the Pitts-Yeager crew was counting on.

It was getting dark when the women returned to the car; the porter had lighted the coach's lamps. The ladies' displays of grief now became downright histrionic. They sobbed and hugged the men so tightly the prisoners' hands disappeared among the billows of their bustled skirts. The quartet passed some twenty minutes in this manner until they finally deemed the time was right.

Manning was the one who saw it. Lambert was gazing out the window and Loring was leaning forward speaking to Gosling, his head momentarily blocking the marshal's view. Pitts' free hand slid out from among the folds of his wife's skirt clutching a pistol. What happened next took place in an instant, which accounts for some confusion among the various accounts. Lambert heard a noise from the aisle, Loring saw a shadow, and both turned to see Pitts and Yeager rising, each clutching a pistol in his free hand. Before anyone could react, Pitts ordered, "Hands up, gentlemen."

Gosling looked at Lambert and said, "Well, I didn't believe they would try it," starting to stand as he spoke. The words were cut off by two pistol shots, and Hal Gosling pitched forward across Lambert's and Manning's laps. Though neither he nor Lambert was certain who fired them, Loring later remembered the shots as striking Manning and Gosling, respectively. All agreed that at least one struck Gosling in the head. Lambert turned him to view his face and noticed that Gosling's lifeless hand gripped the butt of a pistol tucked inside his waistband, snugged under his vest.

Loring came out of his seat shooting. Manning, briefly pinned by Gosling's inert form, quickly got his own pistol into action. The firing then "grew general," as Lambert described it. "The pistol shots were incessant," he said, "and the smoke filled the compartment so densely it was almost impossible to see the forms of the men, and women could be dimly discerned as they sank to the ground." No stranger to gun battles, having served both as a Texas Ranger fighting Indians and a Confederate soldier battling Union troops, Lambert later recalled, "I never heard bullets whistle or hit like they did in that car the night poor Hal Gosling was killed by one of his prisoners."

The two deputies fought side-by-side, the prisoners returning their fire and pressing them in the direction of the ladies' car. A shot from Manning hit Yeager in the neck. Beyond that it was impossible, Lambert said, to tell "who was killed or who was killing." Manning, by now hit in both the neck and shoulder, traded shots until own his pistol was empty. As he backed up a couple of rows and tried to reload, his ejector jammed. A model of cool under fire, Manning squatted down, took a pencil from his vest pocket, and used it to punch out the empty casings. At this point, Lambert, who was unarmed, sought safety in the ladies' car. Loring emptied his pistol and retreated into that car to reload. Meanwhile, Manning had reloaded and come back into the fray. He shot dry a second time, and was falling back to reload again when the two prisoners charged him. Now the fighting became hand-to-hand. Pitts and Yeager thrust their pistol barrels against Manning's body; he just managed to deflect them as they fired, getting his face and coat scorched in the process.

At some point during the skirmish the train's conductor, Charley Fowle, heard the ruckus and came in from the forward car. He was armed with a handgun, and threw in with the deputies. Seeing Mrs. Drown level a pistol in Gosling's direction, then at him, Fowle started shooting, hitting her just below the navel. Rosa Yeager took a stray bullet from someone's pistol and went down.

As Manning fought the two outlaws off, they shoved past him. He was just finishing reloading when Pitts and Yeager wrestled the smoker's rear door open and, with the train still moving at thirty or forty miles per hour, leaped out. The escapees tumbled onto the road bed, clambered to their feet, and disappeared into the trees and the night. As they vanished, a passenger in the ladies' coach, a Colonel Mayfield, snapped a pistol shot out the window, and swore he'd scored a hit.

Loring reentered the smoker just after Pitts and Yeager jumped. Lambert followed. They found the car a bloody mess. Hal Gosling was sprawled across the seats, dead – one bullet hole behind his left ear and another in his back. Manning was bleeding badly from his wounds, and was weakening. Mrs. Drown was gut shot and lay dying, a .45 revolver under her seat. Rosa Yeager had an ugly bullet wound in her right thigh, and Charley Fowle had a bullet crease in his forehead. Lambert later claimed at least fifty shots had been fired in the car. Taking the various statements into account, his estimate is very likely dead on.

Among the combatants Loring alone was uninjured, and he now took charge. Having been a conductor, he knew how to use the pull cord to stop the train. He left Lambert and Fowle to look after the wounded, hopped off, and made a quick but fruitless search for signs of Pitts and Yeager as the train backed up to their approximate jumping-off point. Loring returned, and since it was at this point far from certain who all had taken part in the melee, he and Fowle "made prisoners of the whole Pitts-Yeager 'layout'."

The train double-timed it into New Braunfels, where the injured women received attention and Loring turned his passel of prisoners over to the Bexar County sheriff. Manning was made comfortable in a sleeping car, and he and Lambert took the train, and Gosling's body, on into San Antonio, where they arrived about 11 p.m. Loring stayed behind to organize a posse, which sped off to hunt the escaped convicts. At least two more posses headed out; one was led by Gosling's old friend Texas Ranger Captain Joe Shely, along with Bexar Deputy Sheriffs James Van Riper, Ed Stevens, and Bob Alexander.

Mrs. Drown died later that evening, maintaining her innocence to the last and insisting she'd tried her best to avert bloodshed. Yet there was speculation at the time, and there is some indication from the known facts, that "Grandmother" Drown – not Pitts – put the bullet through the back of Hal Gosling's head. Her positioning was right, given the angle of Gosling's head wound. The slugs found in Gosling were said to be of two different calibers, while the pistols Pitts and

Yeager carried used the same load (weapons could have been mixed up during the fracas or its aftermath). Also, it seems odd that Pitts would give a "hands up" warning, telegraphing his intentions, if he'd planned simply to open fire. If she didn't shoot Gosling, the old warhorse had certainly faced Conductor Fowle like a hardened *pistolero*. So much for Victorian "weaker sex" notions. Before she died, Mrs. Drown asked to be buried alongside her grandson, and she and Pitts were planted side-by-side in New Braunfels the next day.

The Shely posse found Yeager the next morning, several miles from where he and Pitts had bailed out of the train. He had bullets in his neck and shoulder and grudging praise for Manning's marksmanship. Reports described him as "demented" when found, whether from his wounds or the stress of his escape. He led the posse to Pitts' body, lying in a weed patch not fifty yards from where they'd left the train. Pitts' left forearm was horribly mangled and the hand was missing. Seeing no alternative, Yeager had used a sharp rock to separate himself from his pal and make his escape. A lurid newspaper account years later claimed that when the posse captured Yeager, Pitts' gory hand was still dangling from the shackles. The story's wildly farfetched, though it would certainly account for Yeager's shaky mental state.

Yeager made a lengthy, self-serving statement to his captors, placing the blame for the bloody escape on his dead partner. Pitts had smuggled the weapons aboard in his boots, Yeager claimed (no doubt to shield his sister), and had told Yeager, "It's life or death. Help me or I will kill you first, and then fight for liberty." He claimed Pitts had shot Gosling. Yeager did admit that when the shooting started, "I followed suit, keeping up a fire with my left hand," but omitted whether any of his shots had struck home. He was likewise coy about the grisly manner of his parting from Pitts' corpse, stating only that, "I succeeded in wrenching it (the manacle) off of his hand."

The posse intended to take Yeager straight on into San Antonio, but abandoned the plan on learning of "the excited state of feeling" there. Instead, they took him to the jail at New Braunfels where the others, for the same reason, were being held. It was a wise move; Hal Gosling had been well-liked and much respected, and left a wife and two young sons. The *Galveston Daily News* reported that Gosling "was universally popular, and it is safe to say that there is not a decent man acquainted with him that was not his friend." A later dispatch from San Antonio noted that, "Every preparation has been made by the outraged friends of the loved marshal to lynch the prisoners, had they been conveyed here by the night train, as was anticipated. The temper of the people was such that even the women connected with the tragedy would have fallen victims to the wrath of Judge Lynch and his court." By the following day, lynch talk was making the rounds all the way to New Braunfels. The sheriff detailed sixteen deputies to watch over the prisoners and dissuade any such vigilante hijinks.

Meantime, Gosling lay in state at the San Antonio home of his sister, Mrs. W. B. Watkins. Hundreds came to pay their respects. Gosling's funeral at San Antonio on February 23 preempted the city's planned celebrations of Washington's Birthday (the actual holiday falling on a Sunday, the festivities had been scheduled for Monday). Not only had Gosling been popular, he was the first United States Marshal (though many *deputies* had fallen) killed in thirty years. As Lambert recalled, "...the people turned out en masse to show their last tribute of respect to his memory." The *Galveston Daily News* reported that "strong men wept as bitterly as the ladies of the household," but pulled no punches in assigning Gosling partial blame for his death. "It can not [sic], however, be denied," the *News* stated, "that the deplorable tragedy is largely due to Mr. Gosling's own, almost criminal, carelessness."

Gosling's body rode to the Knights of Pythias cemetery in a four-horse hearse. The stately procession included "Mounted police; two companies of the Eighth United States Cavalry; United States Light

Battery of artillery; Eighth Cavalry band, playing the Dead March in Saul; Marshals August Belknap and G.A. Duerler; San Antonio Rifles." Among the pallbearers were Ranger Captain Shely, along with Gosling's fellow attorneys Charles Ogden and Leon Tarleton, both of whom would later assist in the effort to prosecute Yeager and the others for Gosling's murder.

With the marshal buried and his killers either dead or in custody, nothing remained but to bring those being held to trial. A preliminary hearing was set for Friday, February 27, in New Braunfels. The slight delay was probably to accommodate John Manning, who had at first been considered mortally wounded. On February 25 the *Galveston Daily News* reported that Manning was improving but that his doctor, "for the present, refuses to sanction any exciting conversation." The paper did promise "startling developments" at the hearing, saying that Manning's version of the tragedy was expected to "differ materially from any account hitherto made."

The hearing took place as scheduled but without Manning, who was still bedridden. District Attorney Eugene Digges read affidavits before Judge Arcline charging Charles Yeager, Celestine Yeager (Charlie's brother), Rosa Yeager, Mrs. L. Pitts (Melissa), Annie Scott, T.J. Scott, Carroll Brannon, William Hardeman, and Carl and Emile Krant (other members of the Robbers' Cave bunch) with the murder of Harrington Lee Gosling.

Mac Anderson, the Helotes gang's old friend, found himself defending Charlie Yeager again. Anderson waived examination on Yeager's part and entered "not guilty" pleas for all the other defendants. After the pleas were recorded, the people called Deputy Marshal Fred Loring to the stand. Loring gave a fairly straightforward account of the incidents, beginning with Pitts' and Yeager's trial and concluding with Fowle's assisting him in arresting the defendants after the shootings. Will Lambert was sworn next. His testimony was not as detailed or exhaustive as Loring's; he stated that he left the car after the firing commenced and that when he returned Gosling was already dead.

In all, nine prosecution witnesses gave testimony over two days' time. Some of the most interesting – and damning – testimony came from a jailhouse informant aptly named James B. Leak. He was serving a two-year sentence for forgery, and had shared a cell with Pitts and Yeager for several days a few weeks before the murder. Leak testified that Melissa Pitts and Rosa Yeager had visited the two men regularly, and that he'd heard the four of them planning Gosling's killing. He claimed that Mrs. Pitts "was the sole hatcher of the plot," and that she "begged and plead [sic] with her husband and Yeager to make one effort for liberty." Pitts, Leak said, wanted no part of the scheme, but "threatened to commit suicide before murder," and "cried bitterly over (Gosling's) arranged taking off."

By March 28 John Manning was well enough to testify at a habeas corpus hearing before Judge Hurt in San Antonio. Despite the Galveston newspaper's tantalizing predictions, his testimony mainly corroborated that given by Loring and Lambert. The "startling developments" were that Manning bluntly detailed Gosling's errors in judgment, and that he testified he saw Pitts obtain a pistol from his wife. Manning also claimed someone snapped a shot at him from near the front of the car as Pitts and Yeager jumped out, but he couldn't identify the shooter. Despite the testimony and evidence implicating Melissa Pitts, Rosa Yeager, and others of the group, U.S. District Attorney Jack Evans remained skeptical about the case's chances. In an interview with the *Galveston Daily News* he predicted that "unless a death sentence can be procured against Yeager, the attorney general will in all probability order him at an early date to be carried to Illinois and put in the United States prison. The balance of them will never be brought to trial."

Evans proved to be correct. Though Judge Hurt fixed bail for Carroll Brannon and Rosa Yeager, they were unable to pay it. They and the other defendants were bound over for trial in June and a special judge selected (Judge Thomas Paschal, who would normally have heard the case, was Hal Gosling's brother-in-law). Judge L.D. Denman immediately continued the case until December, when it was further continued until June, 1886. In the meantime, a series of events involving the Helotes Gang and their circle eclipsed the Gosling murder, and possibly buried the case for good.

Around the time of the first continuance, Jim McDaniel, another Helotes gang member awaiting a federal prison term for mail robbery, had broken jail in San Antonio. On the first of July he was run to ground and killed in a fierce gun battle with deputy sheriffs James Van Riper and Ed Stevens – both members of the posse that had captured Charlie Yeager. In early August Yeager and Dick Brannon (convicted in March for his part in the Smithwick robbery) made a daring, if short-lived, jailbreak from the county lockup in Austin. Neither made it more than a few hundred yards. A pursuing crowd took after them and quickly cornered Brannon, who, despite being armed with a pistol taken from the jailer, meekly surrendered. Yeager tried to stand off his pursuers with an ax he'd snatched up. When the well-heeled group pointed out the folly of bringing an ax to a gunfight, Yeager conceded the point. The escapees were hauled summarily back to their cells, and shortly afterward Yeager made his long-delayed trip to the federal pen at Chester, Illinois.

Around the first of June 1886, local lawmen got word that Joe Brannon had returned from Missouri. Under indictment in the Gosling murder and suspected in a string of other crimes, Brannon was very much wanted. Deputy James Van Riper and his brother William (also a deputy sheriff) set out for Carroll Brannon's place where they expected to find his fugitive brother. They took along Frank Scott, Melissa Pitts' brother (and a Bexar County constable), to help identify the outlaw. Joe Brannon was indeed there. When confronted, he made a break for cover and began firing on the lawmen. In the hot skirmish that ensued, a well-placed Winchester shot sheared off Brannon's trigger finger. The unfazed outlaw quickly performed the famous "border shift" (he was from Missouri, after all). Passing his gun to his left hand and bracing it with his mangled right, Joe continued blazing away. After swapping a dozen more shots with Brannon, the deputies rushed his position and found the outlaw bleeding to death from a shot through the lungs. The officers tried to elicit a deathbed confession, but Brannon snorted, "I don't give a damn! I'd rather die than to give away any of the gang to be sent to the penitentiary."

Later in June, Frank Scott was himself in irons, indicted for murder. Local handyman Frank Harris had shown the bad sense to court Annie Scott against the express wishes of brother Frank and her brother-in-law, Jim Pitts. Harris had disappeared the previous September. His skeleton was found months later in a pit near Carroll Brannon's property, a bullet hole through the back of the skull. The Harris murder case again involved witnesses from both the Scott and Brannon families, but this time on opposing sides. Ever since Gosling's death, there had been bad blood between the Scotts and Brannons. Mary Brannon (Carroll's wife) was Jim Pitts' sister, and blamed Melissa Pitts and her Scott relations for Jim's death. Carroll blamed Frank Scott for his brother Joe's death. The Brannons were therefore more than happy to testify against Frank Scott. He was convicted and given a life term.

With Joe Brannon and Jim McDaniel dead (to say nothing of Jim Pitts and Grandmother Drown), Yeager, Dick Brannon, and Frank Scott in prison, and the Scotts and Brannons no longer on friendly terms, the Helotes Gang was effectively out of business. Maybe it seemed redundant to spend state resources prosecuting Charlie Yeager and the others now; Yeager was, after all, already facing a ninety-nine year stretch. Pitts was dead, most of the witnesses agreed he'd killed Hal Gosling, and if it was old Mrs. Drown instead – well, Charley Fowle had done for her, too. Whatever the reasoning, Charles Yeager and the others never stood trial for Hal Gosling's murder.

Yeager did time in Chester for the Smithwick post office robbery until December 1903, when an unexpected Christmas gift arrived. Rosa Yeager, now Mrs. Leo Ichter, had for years petitioned Washington for her brother's release. As an eyewitness to Gosling's murder (never mind her part in it, which she neatly sidestepped) she swore that Pitts had fired the fatal rounds. Affidavits from Fred Loring and former Bexar County Commissioner and justice of the peace William Boerner, who'd also been a rider on the death train, bolstered her claim. Her campaign paid off; President Theodore Roosevelt signed the pardon on December 23, and Charles Yeager spent his holidays a free man. He returned to south Texas, vowing "to show his friends that he could and would be a good citizen." He appears to have kept his promise. When Yeager died on January 15, 1931, the San Antonio newspapers mentioned only that he "was a native of San Antonio and was an employee of the city park department." Long forgotten, or maybe forgiven, were Charlie Yeager's lengthy prison term, his hell-bent younger days as a Helotes Gang outlaw, and his role in the murder of a too-decent-for-his-own-good United States Marshal.

Chapter 4: *"The room looked more like a slaughter house than a court of justice."*
Detective John William Gilley
Kansas City, Kansas (May 13, 1889)

Crooks are born, some say, but every copper was something else first. John William Gilley started out in the shoe business. The son of Prussian immigrants, he was born in Clark County, Ohio, in 1852. By 1870 the Gilleys lived in Ottawa, Kansas, where William (as he's listed in early records) worked alongside his father in the shoemaking trade while elder brother Henry was in medical school. He married Caroline "Carrie" Bridge in August of 1871, and by 1880 William and Carrie were raising three sons: Walter, Albert (known to the family as "Bertie") and Harry. They remained in Ottawa, where Gilley was listed as working in a shoe factory. By the 1885 state census (where he was listed as "John") his occupation was given as "clerk." He was a store clerk – a shoe salesman – "one of the best in the country," the local papers said. The census was taken in March; in November Caroline died, and John Gilley was left alone to care for his three young sons.

By the following month, John and his boys were living in Kansas City, Kansas, in an area known as "the Bottoms," and he was working in a new profession – as a patrolman for the Kansas City Police Department. One of the earliest mentions of Officer Gilley in local newspapers had him investigating – chillingly, considering later events – the pocket knife stabbing of a 14-year-old boy. In December 1885, the *Kansas City Star* reported Gilley's arrest of John Hogan for robbery. Gilley developed a knack for catching robbers and burglars, a skill set that enabled him to move up the ranks quickly.

One of Gilley's fellow new hires on the fledging department was James Edgar Porter, who'd go on to distinction in Kansas City as mayor and in Kansas as a state legislator. Porter and his fellow probationer, John Gilley, shared a footbeat in the meatpacking district that straddled the Kansas-Missouri line. Their beat included a block of Ninth Street which Porter called "the wettest in the world," owing to the fact that twenty-three of the block's twenty-four businesses were saloons (at a time when Wyandotte was a dry county). It was prime training ground, and the two rookie coppers learned quickly. After a time the pair began to ponder their career prospects. "What do you think about this job, Gilley," Porter asked his new friend one day. "Is it worth keeping?" When Gilley said he wasn't sure, Porter offered his own opinion. "I'll tell you what I think," he said, "I'm going to try for promotion – promotion or quit." Gilley pledged to do the same and they shook hands on the deal. Eighteen months later, Porter was a sergeant and Gilley was the department's first, and only, detective.

Not long after O.K. Serviss, a fellow native of Clark County, Ohio, was appointed chief of police in 1886, John Gilley found himself in his new assignment. Detective Gilley proved to be a vigorous and able investigator. He developed a network of informants among the area's criminal populace, and quickly became a feared force among Kansas City's underworld types. He built excellent working relationships with his counterparts over the state line on the Kansas City, Missouri, police force; they often found themselves fishing from the same scummy pond. Gilley also formed a fast friendship with his sister agency's police chief, Thomas Speers.

In mid-December 1886, Gilley was assigned to investigate the burglary of a local store and soon settled on his man – local professional "cracksman" Michael Gohn, AKA Ryan. Gilley located Gohn at a Sixth Street saloon, mere yards from the state line, where he found the burglar calmly sipping a beer. With Sgt. Henry Kersey as backup, Gilley entered Jack McCarty's saloon prepared to make the pinch. He wasted no time, but walked directly up to Gohn and said, in his characteristic low-key way, "I guess we want you." Gohn had seen the officers approaching and, no doubt knowing what they wanted, was ready. His hand concealed by the end of the bar, it suddenly flashed into view with a pistol clamped in it. "Well, you won't get me!" Gohn replied as he threw down on Gilley and Kersey. The officers were made of similar stuff; without hesitation, each drew his sidearm and fired two rounds at Gohn. Caught flat-footed after all, Gohn dropped without firing a shot. Both of Gilley's .38 slugs had struck home, while Kersey's .44 Smith and Wesson had scored a single hit. Gohn died in the county jail a couple of weeks later.

Gilley gained a fast reputation as "a terror to burglar and cracksman and confidence man, and the common sneak thief and highway robber feared him as well." With the help of his fellow officers on both sides of the state line, John Gilley spent the next couple of years busting up the gangs of criminals and assorted "toughs" who infested the region. Many of these miscreants were transient types who drifted in and out of Kansas City, often working legitimate jobs at the local meatpacking plants by day, and capering with their crooked pals by night. One of these was a fellow named Tom Lavin, who probably came to Gilley's attention early in 1886 when Lavin and a cohort rolled a drunk along the Santa Fe tracks by the Missouri River and both were sent up for strong-arm robbery. Career criminals, then as now, tended to return to where they had friends and connections and knew the area. Lavin was no exception; within weeks of his release he was back in Kansas City.

Meanwhile, Gilley was kept busy with other matters. In the fall of 1887 his testimony helped convict two meatpacking union strikers of murder for sabotaging railroad tracks and causing a train derailment that killed a man named Horton. Months later he made the papers again when he arrested a local burglar for a break-in at a prominent citizen's home. In March of 1889, he took part in an incident alongside his friend Porter that demonstrates the grit it took to be a policeman in old Kansas City. During a particularly contentious local election, Sgt. Porter received a telephone call that a group of "ward workers" was en route from the Missouri side of the Kaw River with intent to vote in the Kansas City, Kansas, election. Porter had only time to round up Gilley and a patrolman for backup. The three confronted a mob of thirty-five led by "two Missouri alderman" in the street near the polling place. One of the men faced off with Porter, grabbing him by the lapels. Porter instantly whacked the assailant's knuckles with his billy club – the only time in his career he used it – and ordered the mob to disperse and return whence they came, or else. The gang turned back for Missouri "on a run," but only after Gilley and the other officer had "used their clubs to emphasize the sergeant's speech." Shortly afterward, Porter was promoted to captain.

The same month, Gilley was involved in another court case, testifying in the trial of "Red" Quinn for burglarizing a tailor's shop, a case he worked with detectives from Kansas City, Missouri. "Up to adjournment Tuesday," wrote the *Kansas City* (Kansas) *Times*, "it looked like it would be a hard thing to convict Quinn." Gilley's expert testimony, however, made the difference and soon "settled the case."

Gilley's skill and luck didn't hold, however, when it came to another crook named Red – James "Red" (also known as "Reddy") Smith. Smith was a baby-faced thirty-something who had come from Chicago about 1884, as the *Kansas City Star* reported, "in company with John Costello and others, all known to the police to be professional crooks." Smith and Costello were among the others of their ilk who worked the packinghouses. In the 1885 state census, Smith – as did Costello – gave his occupation as "butcher." Both lived in a boarding house run by Jennie Hogan, or they did until April of 1885, when Costello was shot and killed in a quarrel with a newspaper editor over local politics.

Smith, meanwhile, became a familiar face to the Kansas City police, and to John Gilley in particular. Smith was an ex-con said to have served terms "in several of the state prisons of the west" where he had always been "a trouble inmate."

When he wasn't skulking around Kansas City as a small-time robber and burglar, James "Red" Smith worked as a butcher in the city's meat-packing plants. *(Author's Collection)*

A small man – an advantageous trait for a burglar – Smith was later described by Gilley's colleague James Porter as "one of the most desperate men he has ever met." Smith was implicated in crimes across several neighboring states, and had been a member of the "Dirty Dozen" criminal gang that had preyed on Kansas City until, largely through Gilley's dogged efforts, the gang had been scattered to the wind.

Smith himself had been out of circulation since December 1887, when he was convicted of robbery for the impressive crime of stealing a dollar from "an old, one-legged man named Manning." Once again the trouble inmate, Smith tried to escape custody while being transported to prison, but his effort to jump from the train ferrying him up river was thwarted. After serving out his term for the crime, Smith blew back into Kansas City – and his old haunts – in late March of 1889. He apparently couldn't stand to be idle long; on the night of April 17 burglars broke into the offices of the Badger Lumber Company in Armourdale – Kansas City's meat-packing district. Though the safe was "broken open" the take wasn't much – three dollars cash, a check worth $75.00 and a $15 overcoat. A patrol officer arrested Smith in the vicinity later that evening for being drunk in public and resisting.

Detective Gilley set to work on the case. He believed from the outset the job was Red Smith's doing. It bore Smith's trademark: maximum damage and minimal results. Within a week Gilley had gathered sufficient evidence, including sworn statements from his snitch networks, to arrest Smith for the burglary. Gilley collected his man without incident. Smith was arrested, arraigned, and remained in custody in the Wyandotte County Jail pending his preliminary hearing on May 11.

Gilley was confident he would put Smith away. His star witness would be none other than Tom Lavin, who was "known to be associated with Smith in many thieving projects." Lavin was not standing charges for the Badger Lumber job, but Gilley had arrested him on other matters likely to result in a lengthy prison term of his own. Smith had been foolish enough to confide in Lavin about the Badger burglary and – honor among thieves, etc. – Lavin had cut a deal with Gilley. In exchange for lesser charges, Lavin agreed to testify that on the evening of April 17, he had seen Smith stash an overcoat in a trunk in his room and that Smith had admitted he'd pinched the coat in the Badger burglary. Besides Lavin, Gilley had found another Smith associate, James Dumphrey, willing to give state's evidence against his old pal. Some news accounts cite Dumphrey as an employee of Badger Lumber, implying that he was Smith's accomplice in an inside job.

By whatever means, Smith became aware that Lavin and Dumphrey were set to testify against him. It didn't seem to concern him much; he remarked to his attorney that he "guessed the boys wouldn't do him any harm." Curiously, he also informed his lawyer that his services wouldn't be needed at the preliminary hearing. "Gilley had incurred Smith's enmity by working up the case against him," wrote the *New York Times* after the day's events, "and it was upon Gilley's testimony that the prosecution to-day [sic] mainly depended." Smith was all too aware of this. On May 11 Smith was removed from his cell to be transported to the Wyandotte County Courthouse on Minnesota Avenue. The hearing would take place in a second floor courtroom, presided over by justice of the peace John Dean Lewis. Though this was merely a hearing to determine if the case against him should proceed to trial, Smith clearly had no illusions about the outcome. So he had made plans, hinted at by the statements to his lawyer, and made clearer as he was being moved from the courthouse holding cell to Lewis' courtroom just before 2 p.m. Smith then was overheard to remark, "If I could only kill that man Gilley, I would sacrifice my own life."

This was apparently taken by the officers who heard it to be nothing more than con bluster. Sadly, Smith was deadly serious. He was escorted into the courtroom by a constable named Woodruff, one of those who had heard the threats. As Woodruff removed Smith's handcuffs, Smith "talked garrulously and seemed in high good humor." This changed when John Gilley entered along with fellow Kansas City police officer Solomon Meluney. As he spotted Gilley, "Smith scowled at him and his good humor gave way to sullen silence."

Whether or not he was aware of Smith's ominous statements, Gilley seems not to have concerned himself. Preliminary hearings were, and are, normally tame affairs concerned with forms and paperwork and the dry minutia of the legal process – boring stuff for those whose main business is chasing bad men. Gilley's prehearing time was mainly spent conferring with Lorenzo Dow McLain, a private attorney who had been appointed to prosecute the state's case. McLain had not had a chance to review the case and relied upon Gilley to bring him up to speed. The two men repaired to a small, private office in a corner of the courtroom where the detective outlined the case, including his deal to secure Lavin's testimony.

Meanwhile, the other parties in the case were assembled: Judge Lewis at a desk on the south side of the room, Woodruff and Smith on a bench along the wall to the judge's right, Tom Lavin and Sgt. Meluney on another bench further along the wall. In a witness room on the north side of the courtroom, Officer C.E. Reynolds (some reports say George Jillich) waited with a group of seven or eight witnesses – Badger Lumber employees and others. Among these were Smith's turncoat associate James Dumphrey and one Charles Duke, a "weighmaster of the Armour-Dole Elevator Company."

After their briefing session, Gilley and McLain reentered the courtroom and took seats along the right side of Judge Lewis' desk. McLain sat at the corner of the desk to Lewis's immediate right, and Gilley sat at McLain's right, his back to the bench on which Woodruff and Smith sat, six or eight feet away. The somewhat informal proceeding began quietly enough. McLain was reading into the record a list of prosecution witnesses, and when he read out the name "William Grover," Gilley broke in to correct him. "It is William Graver" he said.

At that instant, James Smith quietly stood and crossed the short distance to Gilley, a small object glittering in his right hand. It was a common pocketknife of the type known as a "Barlow" – a folding knife with a blade of only two-and-one-half inches. But Smith's blade was "ground to an edge, keen as a razor's" and he had worked as a meat cutter.

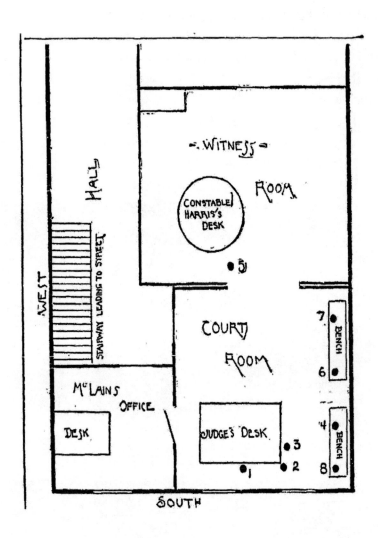

The diagram published in the *Kansas City Times* shows the positions of the key figures, just prior to Red Smith's brutal attack.
Nos. 1, 2, & 3 are the positions of Justice Lewis, Attorney McLain and Detective Gilley. 4 is Smith's position just prior to the attack. 6 Tom Lavin; 7 Sgt. Meluney; 8 Woodruff; 5 where Smith fell. *(Author's Collection)*

Before anyone could realize Gilley's peril or react, Smith struck. Sitting at Gilley's left, focused on the papers before him, McLain's first inkling of the attack was "a sudden stream of blood spurting from Gilley's neck over the papers and his clothing." Judge Lewis was hunched over his desk writing when he became aware of a commotion at his right and heard Gilley say, "Boys, you've killed me." He looked up at the sound to see what, for even a veteran officer of the court, was surely a sight of unimaginable horror. As Meluney later described it, "I have been in many place were [sic] knives and revolvers were used, but never have I witnessed such a terrible scene as this.

Red Smith's weapon was a common "Barlow" pocketknife, similar to this one. How he obtained it, and from whom, was one of the case's great mysteries. *(Author's Collection)*

Without the slightest indication that anything was wrong that man Smith reached over to Gilley and with one stroke cut him from ear to ear."

Smith's experience showed in his stroke. He had plunged the knife down to its bolster in Gilley's neck, just behind the right ear, and cut completely around the right of Gilley's neck to the trachea. As the newspaper reports described – with only slight exaggeration – the wound was "twelve inches long" (later determined to be about seven inches) "and three inches deep, severing all the muscles, gashing the jugular artery [sic] and laying bare the carotid artery."

Time distorts at such moments, and while many things happen at once, they seem to occur in dreamlike slow-motion. Such was the case here. The first thing that happened was that the officers in the room reacted. Woodruff and Meluney were on their feet in an instant, revolvers drawn. At these close quarters, in a tight knot of people, they couldn't risk a shot, so they fought hand-to-hand with Smith, bashing at his head with their sidearms as he slashed at them with his knife. Judge Lewis jumped up and grabbed his chair with momentary thoughts of smashing Smith with it, but wisely backed away instead as the officers grappled with the prisoner.

If Smith – or anyone – thought Gilley was out of action, they had badly underestimated their man, for "by a superhuman effort, he staggered to his feet," pulling his revolver as he rose. His head tipped at a grotesque angle, Gilley joined in the fray; he and his brother officers pummeled Smith. In the midst of the struggle Smith stabbed Meluney in the thigh, an injury the officer only dimly registered in the adrenalin of the moment. At that instant, Smith broke from the officers and started across the room. The officers saw their shot and took it. The *Kansas City Times* wrote that, "Gilley, crimson with his own blood, supported himself against the Justice's desk," and according to Lewis' statements, leaning an arm on the judge himself for support. Gilley "saw his opportunity, and his revolver cracked four times in as many seconds." Woodruff and Meluney fired once or twice apiece; Meluney later estimated that seven or eight shots total had been fired.

When the shooting started, McLain later recounted, "I thought Smith had secured a revolver and to protect myself against stray bullets, I fell to the floor." One shot did in fact injure a bystander; witness Charles Duke received "a painful wound in the leg," the errant slug entering his right thigh "piercing the fleshy part." Despite this mishap, the officers' shooting was effective. As five bullets "found lodgment" in Smith and a sixth grazed him, he staggered to the doorway of the witness room and "dropped like a log."

As the melee ended, the courtroom – which had been "crowded with attendants and visitors" – was now nearly deserted. Some newspaper reports claimed that panicked people had leaped to safety from the second floor windows – unlikely since they'd have had to cross through the thick of the battle to reach the windows. In any case, the room was now strangely empty but for the main players in the tragedy. And even among those, two were conspicuously absent: Tom Lavin and John Gilley. Whether fearing reprisals for his association with Smith or out of guilty involvement in the assault on Gilley, Lavin had taken advantage of the tumult to slip down the adjoining stairway and into the street, to be seen and heard from in Kansas City no more. "And it was lucky for him that he did," reported that *Kansas City Times*, for once word of the bloody doings in the courtroom spread, "Lavin would have been shot on sight wherever found."

As for Gilley, that may have been just what he had in mind. As Judge Lewis checked Smith and saw that he was dead, he noticed that Gilley was gone. As he ducked out to the hall and downstairs to shout into the street for a doctor, the judge witnessed an incredible sight. "Gilley was walking up and down the hall," Lewis later told the *Kansas City Times*, "his revolver still smoking," and it took some convincing on the judge's part to coax the determined lawman back to the courtroom. "He was a terrible sight," said the *Times*. "He was literally running blood and his head was sagging forward in a grotesquely horrible manner." Gilley was still conscious and lucid when they returned to the courtroom, but he was weak from his exertions and from massive blood loss. He asked for his family, and a police patrol wagon dashed off to fetch his sons while a message was sent to his brother and mother in Ottawa. Gilley sat briefly in a chair while Lewis cleared a table for a makeshift bed. Shortly after he was transferred to the table, four local physicians arrived, including Dr. Charles Steman. Though doctors are accustomed to sights that would make the average person swoon, this group was no doubt shocked at the carnage.

"The room looked more like a slaughter house than a court of justice," said the *Kansas City Times,* and it was an apt description.

Smith was shot to pieces. Gilley, Lewis, and McLain were all covered with blood; McLain still clutched the bloodstained legal documents. "The walls and furniture were smeared with blood and a stream of blood trickled across the floor to the hall

A second-floor courtroom in the Wyandotte County Courthouse was the scene of Det. Gilley's horrific murder. *(Author's Collection)*

doorway," the *Times* continued. "Up and down the hall a regular line of blood marked the spot where the detective had staggered after the cutting."

The doctors' prognosis was likewise grim – due to blood loss "and the excitement through which Gilley had passed," they confided to reporters that the detective's odds of survival were one in a thousand.

Meanwhile, the people who'd fled the courtroom chaos and passersby who had seen a gory Lewis calling for doctors had spread the word. While the doctors examined Gilley (and perfunctorily pronounced Smith dead), hundreds of curiosity-seekers converged on the courthouse – so many that the street cars on Minnesota were unable to pass through. The crowd spilled inside the building and soon "half a dozen men could not keep the crowd from the stairway leading to the office."

While the doctors saw to Gilley and treated Meluney and Duke, whose wounds were painful but not life threatening, Smith was loaded onto a stretcher and carried across the street to Swingley & Quarrels, a conveniently-located undertakers' establishment. A post mortem examination revealed that Smith had been penetrated by five bullets – four in the back and one in the abdomen – and grazed along his left rib cage by a sixth. Two of the slugs remained in the body, the others having gone through. "It is thought," reported the *Times*, "that any one of five of the balls would have produced death." The examining doctors credited Gilley with firing three of the solid hits and the grazing shot while Meluney and Woodruff had each hit Smith once. Considering Gilley's severe injury and Meluney's painful leg wound, it was remarkable shooting.

Newspaper reporters were among the first to converge on the scene, and the story quickly went out under sensational headlines. The *Kansas City Times'* front page screamed,

BUTCHERY!
Bloody Tragedy in Open Court – Ghastly Crime of the Notorious Crook "Red" Smith

An Associated Press report went out coast to coast – the *Los Angeles Times* ran the story under "HIS LAST CRIME – Tragic Affair in a Kansas City Courtroom," while the *New York Times* used the more lurid "BLOODSHED IN A COURTROOM," (showing no favoritism for John Gilley, the Gray Lady subheaded its report "A DOUBLE TRAGEDY IN A TEMPLE OF JUSTICE").

This lurid *Kansas City Times* headline gave due credit to Detective Gilley's fortitude, and his marksmanship. (*Author's Collection*)

Once Gilley was stabilized he was moved to his home, where Dr. Steman continued treatment. His horrific wound now sutured and dressed, Gilley "rallied on infusion of salt water into his veins," and was made reasonably comfortable. Dr. Henry Gilley arrived in the evening and took charge of his brother's care. By the following day, John was doing so well that his brother and Steman felt confident of his recovery – so much so that Henry caught an evening train back to Ottawa to see to his own practice. Gilley's mother, meanwhile, remained at a nearby hotel.

Gilley passed the day of May 12 in reasonably good condition, but after nightfall he took a turn for the worse. By midnight, he was so "violently delirious" that his attendants were afraid to give him water. Left briefly unattended, he roused himself from bed and staggered into the adjoining room, apparently looking for his revolver. When his caretakers urged him to return to bed, Gilley snatched up a teacup and "hurled it with great force, aiming at the head of one of those present." He then seemed to calm down, and allowed himself to be led back to bed, but became agitated again and struggled with the attendants to the point that he broke several stitches and began bleeding anew.

He was at last coaxed back into his bed, but continued to worsen throughout the early morning. His sons already present, Gilley's brother was again sent for while a patrol wagon was dispatched to his mother's hotel. Neither arrived in time. Shortly after 9 a.m. on May 13, Gilley's head seem to clear. He recognized a fellow officer, patrolman Robert Thompson, and asked to telephone his old friend from the Missouri side, Chief Speers. The words would be his last. At about 9:30 a.m., with his sons and fellow officers beside him, John Gilley died.

Gilley's body was taken to the Swingley & Quarrels undertaking parlor, where his killer's body still lay. Both would be buried on May 14, but under very different circumstances. Smith would be taken directly to St. John's Cemetery that afternoon, followed by a motley handful of his underworld pals and acquaintances. His remains would not rest there long – after a vigorous protest by the parish priest, his body was disinterred and moved elsewhere.

Gilley would receive the hero's sendoff he deserved. After his body was prepared at the undertaker's it was taken to the downtown home of George Millard, the county coroner, where it would lie in state. Throughout the day and evening of May 13, the house was visited by an unchecked flow of city officials, fellow officers, and citizens of high and low station, who queued up to pay respects to their fallen lawman.

At 8 a.m. sharp on the 14th, the entire Kansas City police force, uniforms brushed and brass buttons gleaming, assembled at City Hall. They were joined by Chief Speers and a "large delegation" of his officers (about twenty-five) from the Missouri side. The two agencies formed ranks and the somber procession marched from City Hall to Millard's house at Fourth and Armstrong Streets. Gilley's remains were placed into a hearse flanked by pall bearers from among his brother officers: Sergeants Thomas Cahill and George Noah, and Officers Robert Thompson, George Jillich, Steven Pilant, and D. Stanley. The hearse was followed by the retinue of officers from both Kansas Cities and their respective chiefs, plus Kansas City Mayor William Coy, postmaster (and Ex-Kansas City police chief) O.K. Serviss, Kansas City's city council and police commissioners, Judge Lewis, and over thirty carriages filled with citizens.

The procession made its way to the Union Depot, where Gilley's casket was placed aboard the Kansas City Southern train that would take it to Ottawa. Kansas City, Kansas Police Chief Petersen ran his day watch with a skeleton crew, allowing twenty-five of his thirty officers to board the train with Gilley's remains. The train pulled into the Ottawa station around noon, met by hundreds of Gilley's friends, fellow officers and citizens. His body was taken to Henry Gilley's home on Hickory Street where the funeral took place at 3:30 p.m.

attended "by the Ottawa police force in a body." Afterward, Gilley's body was taken to Hope Cemetery, where he was buried alongside his wife and father. In an article titled "The Last Roll Call," the *Kansas City Star* wrote that "Detective Gilley's untimely end was mourned as sincerely in Ottawa as in the consolidated cities." Solomon Meluney summed up John Gilley in a few simple words: "I have been with Gilley for a long time and never knew a better officer or a better friend."

The big question in the Gilley case was, of course, how Smith had been able to obtain the murder weapon. Wyandotte County Sheriff Thomas Bowling initially assured the *Kansas City Times* that Smith had been thoroughly searched before leaving the jail for his court appearance. Later statements from sheriff's officials indicated that this may not have been the case. Though it shared in mourning Gilley's death, the Missouri press could not resist allowing a little interstate rivalry to surface. "The dreadful penalty which has resulted in this case of a laxity in vigilance," the *Kansas City Star* wrote, "should impress upon the authorities across the line the necessity of guarding offenders against the law. Such a bloody tragedy as that of Saturday would scarcely be possible in a court of justice on the Missouri side of the river." If Smith had not somehow obtained the weapon while in jail, or in transit, it must have been, the *Star* pointed out, "furnished to him by some of his 'pals' after reaching the courtroom. Even this assumption however would argue a lack of precaution and indicates that there was in some way a neglect of official duty."

Officials would never determine where or how Smith obtained the knife, though most believed he'd been given it while in the courtroom. The two most likely suspects were Smith's disloyal associates, Tom Lavin and James Dumphrey. This could explain Smith's cryptic comment about "the boys" doing him no harm, and would certainly explain the quick exit and disappearance of Lavin who was, after all, only a witness. Dumphrey had likewise joined the mad rush for safety during the Gilley attack, though he proved easier to find. A Kansas City police sergeant arrested him in an Armourdale saloon the morning of May 13. Dumphrey apparently "showed great fear when he was arrested," but denied supplying the knife. Smith claimed Dumphrey, "would have killed him also for testifying against him if he had had a chance." The sergeant phoned Chief Petersen to inform him of the arrest, but there being as yet no evidence against Dumphrey, Petersen ordered him released. Later in the day, when more information was in hand, Officer Stanley and Constable Harris arrested Dumphrey and brought in another Smith associate, a one-eyed man named John Leyden. Both were summarily arraigned before Judge Lewis as accessories to Gilley's murder. Lewis continued the case until after the coroner's inquest on Gilley's death scheduled for May 16. Meanwhile, John Malone, another witness who had fled the Gilley murder scene, was arrested the evening of the detective's funeral on suspicion of having supplied the weapon to Smith.

On the evening of May 21, the coroner's jury returned a sealed verdict which was ordered embargoed until after Dumphrey's preliminary hearing the following week. "While the police will give one nothing," complained the *Wichita Daily Eagle*, "it is believed that they are holding Dumphrey as a blind, and that the real man they are after is Tom Lavin, Smith's Chicago pal, who escaped the courtroom as soon as the shots were fired." If so it was for nothing – Lavin was never found and Dumphrey never tried. A month following Gilley's death three local tramps and small time burglars – Joe A."Frenchy" Young, John Barnes and J.A. Ferrest – were briefly touted as suspects. The three were in jail for burglarizing a railroad freight car. Though all three were Smith associates, and Young had been in jail at the same time as Smith, there was insufficient evidence to make a case against them. In the following weeks several other suspects were questioned and/or arrested but the identity of Smith's accomplice would remain a mystery. Dumphrey was released only to go across the river and be pinched by Kansas City, Missouri detectives on an outstanding warrant for a $20 theft.

While the fruitless search for Smiths's cohort was ongoing, Gilley's department and his city did what they could for his children. "Aside from the $300 they will receive from the Police Relief Association," wrote the *Kansas City Star*, "a fund of over $100 has already been subscribed." The *Star* assisted in the efforts on May 14 stating, "JMS sends the Star $1.00 for the orphan children of Detective Gilley and hopes that others will do the same." A benefit performance at the Ninth Street Theater was scheduled, and on Decoration Day (what today is called Memorial Day) officers of the Wyandotte County court played a judges vs. attorneys baseball game to benefit Gilley's sons. An estimated 6,000 people showed up to watch the judges trounce the lawyers 28-16 and to support the three Gilley boys.

The city fathers looked after the welfare of Gilley's sons by giving the elder two employment. Sixteen-year-old Harry, an expert penman and "typewriter," was hired as clerk for the police court. It must have been a bit unsettling to do much of his work in the very room where his father had been brutally murdered. Walter, aged twelve, went to work as "telephone watchboy" at fire department headquarters.

Harry Gilley's name would appear regularly in the city newspapers in connection with his job as court clerk. He seems to have coped fairly well with his circumstances. His younger brothers, Walter and Albert, went through a troubled phase after their father's death, which threatened to lead them down the same dark path as those Gilley had hunted down through his brief career. By the middle of 1895, Harry was working for the Swift and Company meat packing firm and had transferred to one of its plants in California. Walter and "Bertie," now aged eighteen and sixteen, had been "less fortunate and have since wandered about the country," the *Kansas City Times* reported. Their hoboing had brought them back home to Kansas but it was not a happy homecoming.

In October, a deputy sheriff from Johnson County, Kansas, came to Kansas City for a courtesy call on former police chief, and John Gilley's old friend, O.K. Serviss. Gilley's younger sons, it seemed, had burglarized a citizen's home near Shawnee Mission, Kansas. Both were in jail at Olathe awaiting trial for burglary. In a touch of irony, they were accused of stealing an overcoat. "Chief Serviss and several other friends of the dead detective," wrote the *Kansas City Journal*, "will endeavor to save the two boys from the penitentiary."

In November the pair pleaded guilty to burglary. Whether it was the intervention of John Gilley's friends, the current zeal for prison reform, or the fact that Walter and Bert were orphans with no prior police records, Judge Burris sent them to the recently opened Kansas City Industrial Reformatory in lieu of a prison term. The experience seemed to set them back on the straight and narrow; a decade later all three Gilley boys were married men. Harry had married in 1896; the 1900 census shows him living with wife Bessie in St. Louis. Walter married in Kansas City, Kansas, in December 1905. By 1920, Albert, the youngest Gilley, had six children and was working as a tailor in Wichita.

Gilley's brother officers, meanwhile, moved onward and upward. By the end of 1899, his old friend Tom Cahill was the department's new detective; by the following year Cahill had been named chief of the detective bureau with George Jillich as his assistant. Only days after Gilley's death, Woodruff survived another near brush with death when he was threatened with a double-barreled shotgun while enforcing a lien on a pair of mules. Fortunately, the incident ended peacefully. Meluney recovered from his injury and continued as a Kansas City P.D. sergeant. When he died in Kansas City in 1910, the Gilley killing was mentioned – inaccurately – in his obituary. Gilley's old friend James Porter remained captain until 1901, when he was elected highway commissioner. He served a term as Wyandotte County Sheriff from 1906-1909, and in 1910 was elected mayor of

Kansas City, Kansas. Shortly after his election, Mayor Porter warmly recalled his fellow probationer Gilley in a lively interview with the *Kansas City Star*. Porter smiled as he recounted how they had discussed, when rookies, whether the job was "worth keeping," and decided to seek advancement. When asked what had become of Gilley, Porter's countenance changed, and his mood turned dark. Gilley, he said, "was murdered by a safe blower. The scoundrel cut his throat."

For all his firsts – first Kansas City detective, first Kansas City officer killed in the line of duty – John Gilley was neither the first nor the last, but only the latest, fallen officer quickly forgotten by the community he served. On Decoration Day, 1895, just six years after his death, the *Kansas City Journal* ran a brief page six item stating that the Police Relief Association had sent "a beautiful wreath of flowers" to Ottawa, "to be placed on the grave of Henry Gilley." This must have been quite a surprise to John Gilley's brother, the doctor, who was still in robust health. Nearly as bad as this gaffe was the paper's highly inaccurate account of the events in Judge Lewis' courtroom back in May of 1889.

Gilley was largely forgotten in the years after, eventually even by his own police department. This may have been due in part to the reorganization of the Metropolitan Police; today's Kansas City Police Department traces its history only back to 1898. Kansas City P.D.'s own memorial omitted Gilley's name until 1995, when the oversight was brought to the agency's attention by local historian Loren L. Taylor. Likewise, the Kansas State Memorial, which had overlooked Gilley until 1997. In a ceremony at the Kansas Statehouse on May 23, 1997 – just over 108 years after his death – John W. Gilley and several other Kansas officers had their names added to the roll of 202 already engraved on the monument. Presiding over the long overdue tribute, Gov. Bill Graves addressed the assembled crowd, "Few professions," he said, "have as much honor as those of the men and women who put their lives on the line to make our communities a

safer place. Their only reward is that they have made a difference."
For a man like John William Gilley, that was probably reward
enough.

**This sketch of Detective John Gilley accompanied the *Kansas City Times'*
front-page account of his killing. *(Author's Collection)***

Chapter 5: *"I would like to see my lawyers before I talk any further of the matter."*
City Marshal James F. Isbell
Bells, Texas (January 17, 1891)

Bells wasn't much more than a way station along the Texas Pacific railroad line in northeast Texas. Originally called Dugansville, it was about midway between Dennison and Dallas, and thirteen miles east of Sherman, the Grayson County seat. But it evidently had business enough, and crime enough, to warrant a town marshal. Like many such small town law dogs, Jim Isbell needed more than his paltry pay from the city to make ends meet, so he filled the gaps in his time and his pocket by tending bar at Reisenberg's Saloon, attached to the Union Pacific Hotel. It probably paid off for Isbell in more ways than one. A saloon in such a burg tended to be a hub of activity, catering as it did both to locals and those with time to kill while passing through. It would have made an ideal listening post for keeping up with local happenings. The downside was that it also attracted its share of crime, which is exactly what happened on the night of January 14, 1891.

Between 8 p.m. and 10 p.m. (accounts differ) Isbell was tending bar for a handful of locals while U.G. Keener ran the lunch counter. Patrons included three white men – W.D. Elliott, Jim Hummel and James Matthews – along with two local black men – John Martin and John Hill. It was a quiet, uneventful Wednesday evening. Most of the patrons were grouped around the stove to fend off the winter chill. Elliott and Hummel played a friendly game of dominoes. The restful atmosphere changed when a stranger strode through the door, the .45 revolver in his hand announcing his intention before he spoke a word.

"Throw up your hands," Keener would later quote him as saying, "I ain't got long to stay. I want what money you have." The quick-thinking Keener pulled his money from his pocket and, as he stood, dropped it to the floor and nudged it under the stove with his boot. He and the others stood with upraised hands as the robber trained his gun on Isbell and ordered him to open the saloon safe. Isbell protested that the safe was broken and "pulled out the pin" to prove that this was so.

"There's money here," growled the robber, "and money is what I want." He moved to the end of the bar, keeping his gun trained on Isbell and darting glances at the others to detect and deter any skullduggery. He waved Isbell behind the bar, made him empty the till onto the countertop, then shepherded him back to the crowd near the stove, where he demanded the men produce their watches. Elliott's fine watch caught the robber's eye. "A man who owns such a watch has money," said the bandit. He ordered Elliott to place it on the billiard table. He then directed Martin to search Elliott for money and other valuables. This provided the distraction Isbell needed. As Keener discreetly watched, Isbell reached behind the bar for a holstered pistol. As he pulled the pistol, the scabbard fell to the floor. Isbell put a foot on the holster to hide it but he was too late – the robber had seen the suspicious movement and swung his gun back on Isbell.

"God damn you," he said, "throw up your hands or I will shoot you." Isbell raised his gun and the two men fired almost as one, so close together that witnesses could never agree on who'd fired first. Isbell's quick shot, unfortunately, missed its mark. The robber, who proved himself then and afterward to be cool-headed and nerve-steady, had better luck. His single .45 round, the local paper later reported, "took effect in the right side of Isbell's face, completely shattering the bones of the jaw and coming out the back of the neck and producing an ugly wound which will in all probability prove fatal."

As Isbell dropped to the floor, Keener seized the assailant in a bear hug and the others rushed in and tried to restrain the furiously struggling gunman. Keener just managed to wrench the pistol from his hand before the man broke free and fled through the saloon's west door. As he ran toward the train depot, both Keener and Elliott snapped off shots at him – Keener emptying the bandit's own gun. But the robber's luck held; no bullet hit home. Martin dashed out in pursuit of the robber and caught up with him as he reached the depot. "Martin pursued and overhauled him," reported the *Galveston Daily News*, "and held him until help arrived, when he was secured and brought back." Keener and the others ran to Martin's aid and helped escort the robber back to the saloon

The Union Pacific Hotel housed Sam Reisenberg's saloon, which George Smith entered a robber and exited a murderer. *(Photo courtesy of the Grayson County, Texas GenWeb)*

Whatever means of persuasion Martin had used to detain the bandit, it was mild compared to what the men in the saloon now contemplated. As the *Sherman Daily Register* said, "Isbell was lying in a very weak condition," and as a result, "indignation ran very high and for a while it looked like the crowd was going to avenge the shooting of the town marshal by indulging in a lynching bee." Fortunately for the shooter, "cooler heads prevailed and the prisoner was place under guard." The robber didn't say much except to identify himself, when asked, as "Jim Smith." He'd later claim that his first name was George. Whether true or not, George Smith was the name he would stick with until the very end.

The men summoned a doctor, and under his direction carried Isbell to his home nearby. The plan was to hold Smith until morning, when a deputation of local men would take him into Sherman and hand him over to the Grayson County sheriff.

By the next morning, Isbell was still "lying in a very critical condition" and sinking fast. He was not expected to survive. Smith had lasted the night only because Isbell's condition was uncertain. According the *Dallas Morning News*, the delay in the proposed lynching, "was because of a desire to see how the wound resulted." But once word of Isbell's gloomy prognosis got out, lynch fever spread and mob rule threatened to take over. A "semi-official" message was fired off to Sherman, warning that "an infuriated crowd was threatening to take the prisoner out of the hands of the local authorities and hang him to the first convenient tree." In response, Grayson County Sheriff R. L. McAfee and a deputy named Creagher boarded "the first convenient train for Bells." A brief comedy of errors resulted; while McAfee and Creagher were en route, three Bells locals – "Professor" Riley, Paul McDonald and Jim Buchanan – had started riding towards Sherman with George Smith bound and in custody. The Bells party arrived in Sherman about 1:30 p.m. and turned their prisoner over to sheriff's men at the county jail on Houston Street, where a Deputy Callahan searched him and found a "pistol-holster and a cartridge of .45 calibre [sic]." McAfee and Creagher returned post haste, having received the story from the witnesses at Bells, and Smith's pistol from U.G. Keener.

Though McAfee had not been on hand to greet the posse from Bells, they found a *Dallas News* reporter waiting, eager to interview them and Smith. As none of the possemen had witnessed the shooting, they weren't able to add much to the initial reports. Smith had apparently arrived in Bells from Sherman, they said, sometime the previous afternoon, and had loitered about Reisenberg's saloon from then on. He'd bought no drinks, only several cigars. His odd behavior had attracted the notice of James Matthews, who'd remarked on it to the saloon occupants not a half hour before Smith's robbery attempt. By now other details – and rumors – were circulating in Sherman. Smith had reportedly bought his pistol in Sherman on the 13th, then had hopped a freight train into Bells the following day around midday. It was rumored that Smith was nursing a grudge because he'd lost a goodly amount of money gambling at Reisenberg's. It was later found that though he had frittered away most of his cash at the tables in Sherman on the 13th, he had not gambled in Bells.

For Smith's part, he wasn't talking much – at least about his crime. He offered up few personal details besides a name. He claimed to be a native of Michigan and said that he'd lived in Texas since about 1885, having worked as a farmer all that time. He was said to live "near Choctaw on the Kentuckytown Road," a few miles out of Sherman. "This is the first snap I ever got into in my life," Smith told the Dallas reporter, "and there is not a soul in the world can bring a thing against me." He refused to speak about what had taken place at Reisenberg's saying, "I would like to see my lawyers before I talk any further of the matter."

Throughout the day in Bells, an "anxious crowd hovered outside Isbell's home," wrote the *Sherman Daily Register*, many of whom "went up to take a look at the poor mangled disfigured face and listened to his laborious breathing." Swelling around Isbell's wound had "prevented further outward bleeding," and there was a growing danger of septicemia.

A hopeful sign came the morning of the 16th when the *Sherman Register* received a terse message from Sheriff McAfee: "Jim is some better today we think." This optimism was short lived, however. By the following day, Isbell's wound had become septic and he was acknowledged to be dying.

His assailant, whose preliminary hearing was being postponed until authorities knew whether to charge robbery or murder, was still keeping mum. "Smith remains reticent and does not commit himself pro or con in the matter," reported the *Dallas Morning News*. Smith was not idle, however. From his jail cell he "deeded back to the original owner" thirty acres of farmland he had recently put a deposit upon, and also "mortgaged a pair of horses." Presumably this was to pay anticipated legal expenses, though it may also have crossed Smith's mind that he wasn't going to need land or horses for a long time, if ever.

By this time more information was emerging about Isbell's shooter, who the *Dallas News* stated, "is now recognized by a great many citizens who could not place him at first." Reports said that Smith was a young man in his early twenties, "modestly dressed, does not appear to be a man much given to dissipation and hardly looks the man who would undertake what he came pretty near being successful in last night if reports are true." Smith claimed not to know Isbell and "appeared rather nervous" when mentioning his victim's name. Though jail deputies told the *Dallas News* that Smith had admitted buying his pistol at Roberts, Willis & Taylor Company – a Sherman hardware store – on January 13, Smith vociferously denied this to the press. In checking with the hardware merchants, reporters were unable to verify the purchase.

It was learned that since coming to the Sherman area several years back Smith had worked at several farms, including a dairy farm south of town owned by W.P. Gunn, and a spread near Kentuckytown owned by John and W. T. Dyer. Smith had told his employers he hailed from a "small logging camp" in Michigan. J.D. Moon, with whom Smith had roomed shortly after moving to the area, supported this claim. Moon recalled letters addressed to "George Smith" from a woman in Michigan who Smith claimed was an aunt. When the letters stopped coming, Smith told Moon that the aunt had died. As to Smith's character, Gunn considered him "an energetic hard worker, but a trifle high-tempered," while the Dyers said Smith was, "industrious and attentive to his work, but a little inclined to wish his own way." High praise indeed.

On January 17 the *Sherman Register* reported a phone message received from Bells stating that Marshal Isbell was "surely and steadily sinking. There was a change for the worse last night and this morning found him much weaker and all symptoms go to indicate that he cannot hold out much longer." That evening, Marshal James Isbell succumbed to his injuries. The *Sherman Daily Register* carried the solemn news that, "Saturday night between 8 and 9 o'clock James Isbell, the wounded town marshal of Bells, died from the effect of a pistol shot wound inflicted on him Wednesday night."

The news was tragic, but expected, and no time was wasted now in setting in motion the legal machinery to bring Isbell's killer to justice. C.J. Hinkle, Grayson County Justice of the Peace, went immediately to Bells and convened an inquest. It was a cut and dried proceeding, with testimony from Keener, Elliott and Matthews, along with doctors King and Deatherage who had assisted Dr. Steman in attending Isbell. "The evidence adduced," reported the *Dallas News*, "does not vary to any great extent from what has already been published in The News Friday morning." Hinkle's verdict, rendered on the 19th, likewise surprised no one. "That on the 14th day of January, AD 1891, one George Smith did shoot the said deceased with a pistol inflicting upon the face of the deceased...a pistol shot wound from which said wound the deceased died on January 17th, 1891, about 9 o'clock p.m."

Isbell's funeral took place in Bells on the 18th. "Everybody in the entire town was present," wrote the *Sherman Register*, "eager to show some last token of respect to the man who had lost his life in defense of the law." The family was represented by Isbell's "old mother and the two little nieces," and his fellow lawmen attended en masse. "All the town and precinct officers were present," the *Register* reported, as well as "several officers from the neighboring towns and precincts." Sheriff McAfee himself stood at the head of the pall bearers. The *Register* gave Marshal Isbell a fitting eulogy: "Neither men, women, or children, white and colored, tried to repress the feelings of sorrow that swelled up in their breasts. They all knew James Isbell and loved him; it was not considered a mark of weakness in that sorrowing little town to weep over his dead form."

One man likely numbered among the grieving throng was John Martin, the black man who had pursued and apprehended George Smith. A few years earlier Martin had served a short prison term for bigamy due to his having – apparently inadvertently – remarried without first securing a legal divorce. Due to his ex-convict status, Martin had also lost his right of suffrage. His courageous actions in the Isbell tragedy had not gone unnoticed, however, and the small community of Bells now rallied around him. Though the "rather bashful" Martin was reluctant to discuss the matter, he was "presented with quite a handsome purse by the citizens of Bells." At the same time, a petition seeking pardon, signed by "every man in Bells," was sent to Texas Governor James "Big Jim" Hogg. Based upon the detailed reports of Martin's bravery, Hogg immediately granted him an unconditional pardon and restored his citizenship rights.

George Smith was indicted for first degree murder. He would have an able defense attorney in James D. Woods, a prominent local lawyer who'd practiced law in Grayson County for over thirty years, and had served terms as district attorney and as mayor of Sherman.

Woods had been captain of a dismounted cavalry unit in the Confederate army, and would be ever after known to his fellow Texans as "Captain" Woods.

Since the evidence against Smith was quite compelling – a room full of reliable eyewitnesses all giving the same account of what happened – Captain Woods was forced to take a different tack. Smith admitted outright to Woods that he had entered Reisenberg's saloon with robbery in mind, but denied that he'd intended to kill anyone. Woods knew that even if

Captain James D. Woods
(Author's Collection)

that were true it might not save his client from the noose. Under Texas law, killing in the course of robbery was still first degree murder. So Woods chose to plead that his client was insane, and thus not responsible for his crimes. Smith's actions on the day in question had certainly been odd for a man hoping to get away with robbery. He'd loitered about the saloon all day, entered it more than once, had even spoken face-to-face with Keener, the prosecution's star witness. He'd ridden a freight train into town and presumably had no better escape plan than hoping to catch one back. Still, stupid was one thing and insane another.

Yet Woods' strategy worked to a point; the trial jury retired for deliberation on April 11, but by the 14th found themselves unable to return a verdict. The *Fort Worth Gazette* declared them "A Badly Hung Jury," and reported that the group has deadlocked at "six for hanging, five for life and one for acquittal." The latter juror, it seems, had bought the insanity defense. Judge P.B. Muse had no alternative but to declare a mistrial and dismiss the jury.

Both of George Smith's trials for Marshal James Isbell's murder took place at the Grayson County Courthouse in Sherman. *(Author's Collection)*

The case was called for trial again on May 26. Public interest in the matter remained high; the *Dallas Morning News* reported that at 10 a.m. "there was a large crowd in the district court room [sic] to witness the trial of George Smith for the killing of Town Marshal Isbell at Bells in January last." Again the crowd was destined for disappointment. This time Woods sought a continuance on grounds that a crucial insanity defense witness, Mrs. John Dyer (wife of Smith's former employer), was ill and unable to attend. After sending a doctor and a deputy sheriff to the Dyer home and verifying this, Judge Muse granted the continuance and trailed the case until the fall term. The road to acquittal was long and unsure, but Woods had at least bought his client a few more months.

While he remained in jail awaiting his new trial, Smith's "first snap in his life" statement was soon called into question when a St. Louis Southwestern Railway detective named Byrnes came to Sherman on the trail of a train robber. On December 1, 1890, a lone gunman had robbed a train on the railway's "Cotton Belt" line near Pittsburgh, about seventy miles southeast of Sherman. The bandit, a ticketed passenger, had uncoupled the coach he was riding in while the train was in transit. As the train vanished into the night, leaving the coach behind, the man pulled a pistol and began robbing the stranded passengers. His caper went smoothly until he reached "an old gentleman by the name of J.H. Gearhardt." Gearhardt "showed fight" and grappled with the robber, who shot him twice through the lungs. But Gearhardt was a tough Texan; the *Fort Worth Daily Gazette* reported that after being shot, he "threw the desperado from the car and shut the door." The hapless bandit fled minus the hat and cravat he'd lost in the scuffle, stopping only long enough to rob a railroad line worker and steal his hat.

Byrnes had obtained affidavits from Gearhardt – who had survived his wounds – and the railroad worker, Shackleford. Both identified George Smith as the train robber, and Byrnes told the *Dallas News* he expected to have a complaint filed within a few days. But the Texas courts preferred to finish dealing with Smith on the capital case first, after which the Cotton Belt train robbery would, with any luck, be a moot point.

On November 4, George Smith's delayed case was called for trial. Woods' first action was to request a change of venue, claiming that local prejudice against Smith would prevent a fair trial. "After considerable argument, pro and con," reported the *Dallas Morning News*, "the court finally set aside the application and the trial went on."

The court heard two days of testimony from Keener, Elliott and the others who had seen Isbell shot. This included testimony that Smith had been in the saloon earlier that day when Reisenberg had openly described plans to go to Sherman the next day, carrying several hundred dollars to renew his liquor license. In the end, the prosecution had stated its case clearly and done its best to discredit Woods' insanity defense. The jury went into deliberation the afternoon of November 6. By 11 a.m. the following morning, they had a verdict.

Throughout both trials, newspaper reports had made much of Smith's cool, unruffled demeanor. This morning was different. "The prisoner," wrote the *Dallas Morning News*, "who has always displayed a good deal of indifference, now looked a little nervous." He had good reason. The jury foreman handed the verdict to the court clerk, who read out its concise nineteen-word message: "We the jury find the defendant guilty of murder in the first degree and assess his punishment at death."

Smith's nonchalant airs vanished entirely. He loudly cursed Judge Muse, the gentlemen of the jury, and reserved "some very violent epithets" for Sheriff McAfee, whom he accused of perjury. He was immediately remanded to custody and returned to the county lockup where he made petulant refusals to talk to any reporters. No matter – the jubilant headline in the next day's *Fort Worth Gazette* shouted, "SMITH WILL HANG," followed by the more cautious subheadline, "At Least the Jury Said He Ought to be Hanged."

Woods wasted no time after the verdict. Just over two weeks later, on the 23rd, he again stood before Judge Muse to move for a new trial. An affidavit from one M.H. Kempton – a cellmate of Smith's while he was awaiting trial – would, Woods claimed, offer new evidence supporting the contention that Smith was insane.

The prosecution asked time to file controverting affidavits, so Muse continued the matter. Two weeks later on December 7, Muse issued his ruling. Since the defense presumably had access to

Kempton's information – whatever it was – at the time of Smith's trial, and had not done due diligence in obtaining and presenting it, the court would not now recognize it as "newly discovered evidence." In short, there would be no new trial; the verdict would stand. Woods instantly filed a notice of appeal.

Smith's case went before the Texas Court of Criminal Appeals in April of 1892. A three-judge panel consisting of Justices James Hurt, E.J. Simkins and W.L. Davidson heard Woods' arguments against the Smith verdict, while Assistant Attorney General R. H. Harrison presented the state's case. Woods' first point of appeal claimed ambiguity in Muse's mention of "express malice" in his instructions to the jury; the indictment had charged Smith with killing Jim Isbell "with malice aforethought." Secondly Woods raised the question, as he'd already done at trial, as to who fired first on January 14 – Isbell or Smith. Next he contended that Muse had erred in telling the jury that the defense's claims of Smith's insanity must be "clearly proven," when the law required only a preponderance of evidence. Woods' final two points questioned whether Muse had erred in denying a change of venue, and in refusing to grant another trial.

On April 27, the judges handed down their decision (written by Davidson). The appellate court found no fault with Muse's ruling on any score. Among other points, Davidson declared that whether Isbell or Smith had fired first was immaterial. If it was Isbell, he was lawfully attempting to prevent a robbery, and for Smith's part it was first degree murder either way.

On the morning of April 29, Captain Woods dropped by his client's county jail cell to deliver the bad news in person. "Well, Smith," he said "the Court of Appeals have affirmed your case." If Smith was insane, he hid it well. "Yes, I've been expecting that for some time," he replied with a wry smile. His unflappable manner renewed, Smith asked when his execution date was likely to be. When Woods told him that formal sentencing was still several days off and the date would be set for at least thirty days beyond that, Smith seemed disappointed. He grumbled that he didn't "see why they should be so long about it."

Then tallying on his fingers, he brightened and said, "That will throw it into warm weather which will be nicer." Woods said he would do his best to have Smith's hanging held on a different day from that of Sam Massey, awaiting execution in a notorious rape/attempted murder case which had largely overshadowed the Isbell murder in the press. Smith was unconcerned. "That hole out there isn't hardly large enough to drop more than one through," he said. It was no matter, anyway; Massey's own court appeals would delay his death for another year. Smith told Woods he "didn't care to see a preacher." He had a Bible, he said, but requested some magazines, saying he had "read so many novels he was sick of them."

Smith received a little extra reading time; his sentencing was delayed until May 20, when he was led into Judge Muse's courtroom by his old friend Sheriff McAfee. Before pronouncing sentence, Muse called for quiet and made a surprise announcement. Once again the Massey case threatened to eclipse Isbell's murder as Muse informed a packed and stunned courtroom that he was granting a change of venue to Massey "for his own safety." Several weeks earlier a mob of around five hundred armed men had stormed the Houston Street jail with their own change of venue in mind – to the court of "Judge Lynch." McAfee and jailer McKinney had anticipated this. They had sneaked the prisoner out of town just ahead of the mob, which nonetheless commandeered the jail keys and conducted a top-to-bottom search. Massey was safely installed in the Dallas County jail at the time of Muse's announcement.

In transferring the case elsewhere, Judge Muse was likely more concerned with the safety of McAfee and his men than with Sam Massey's. His announcement was not met with pleasure. "The courtroom was still as the tomb," said the *Galveston Daily News* "and faces that looked stern at Smith now looked with compassion, perhaps it was a comparison of the two crimes. Smith had killed an able bodied man, but Massey most brutally assaulted, endeavored to murder a family and tried to burn the house with occupants, every one of whom he left in an insensible condition." The public – or the minions of the press, anyway – seemed suddenly to have forgotten Jim Isbell's sacrifice.

If so, Judge Muse hadn't. He ordered Smith to stand, gave a terse recitation of his crimes and the course of his case through trials, motions and appeal, then asked if there was any reason the court should not pronounce sentence. "The prisoner looked the court squarely in the face," wrote the *Galveston Daily News*, and answered, "No sir." Muse, at last, had the final word. "It is then my duty," he went on, "to remand you to the custody of the sheriff, to be held by him until Friday, the 8th of July, when within the hours prescribed by law, you shall be hanged by the neck until dead." The formalities observed, Smith was escorted from the room with "a clanking of chains and a rattling of shackles," and taken back to his jail cell "to drag out the six weeks of life left to him."

As Smith's sentencing date drew near he seems to have rethought his stance on preachers. The *Dallas Morning News* reported that on May 9 Smith "courteously received Rev. J.A. Ivey, pastor of the Second Baptist church." After the two engaged in "quite a consultation" and "a fervent prayer," Ivey took his leave. Smith invited him to visit again, saying, "I believe you are really interested in me and did not come just out of curiosity, as so many have done."

Besides Woods' energetic defense, there were also the usual sort of grassroots efforts to spare Smith from the noose. In early May Texas Governor Hogg received a letter asking that he commute Smith's sentence to life behind bars. Hogg gave enough consideration to the appeal that he wrote the Grayson County Court requesting a copy of the judgment, and even visited Bells, where he was shown the scene of the crime. The day after Smith's sentencing the *Galveston*

Daily News reported that a petition for commutation was being circulated, but that a counter petition to let the sentence stand "signed by nearly everybody in Bells and vicinity" had been placed in the governor's hands during his visit. "His Excellency of course," the paper remarked, "said neither yea nor nay."

Less than a week before his execution date, George Smith's last chance at clemency vanished. After having considered the petitions and reviewed all the facts of the case, including a written statement from Grayson County Attorney Cecil H. Smith, Governor Hogg declined to intervene. Just under a year and a half since he'd killed Marshal James Isbell, George Smith was going to hang.

The *Galveston Daily News* began covering the pending event on July 7. Under the headline, "HIS LAST NIGHT," it said, "George Smith entered upon his last night on earth with all the calm exterior that he has evinced since the very beginning." Both the Galveston and Dallas papers printed in-depth coverage, based on the same dispatch, the morning after. While the *Dallas News* devoted several column inches to the "History of the Crime," the Galveston paper allotted Isbell's death only cursory mention. In a brief sentence at the end it said merely, "In January 1891, Smith killed City Marshal Isbell of Bells while trying to hold up a whole store." Isbell literally had become a footnote in his own story.

The papers each spent the bulk of their narratives on detailed, sickeningly sympathetic accounts of Smith's final hours. The *Dallas News* made much of Smith's "prepossessing" appearance, "fine chin and lip" and his "well-proportioned" chest and shoulders. "His face denoted determination," it went on, "yet withal lacked the usual cast of the criminal."

Both newspapers' accounts began by pointing out that Smith would be the first person hanged in Grayson County since 1879, when Julius Toetel murdered Joseph Brenner. The Toetel case bore curious parallels to the Smith case; Brenner was murdered in a Denison saloon where he worked, and he was killed on January 15 (Smith shot

Isbell on January 14). At trial both were alleged insane, both verdicts were upheld upon appeal, and in both cases sympathetic citizens submitted petitions to commute the death sentences. In another day would come the final similarity – both killers would have been hanged for their crimes.

Smith's last night was well documented by both papers. He ate supper "with apparent relish" and whiled away the evening talking with the "death watch" and his cell mate Henry Garbutt, who awaited trial as part of a Canadian check forgery ring. The only indication that this night was different than any other was Smith's occasional casual remark, "Well, this is my last night here." Smith turned in about 11 p.m. and "his rest was practically unbroken" until 7 o'clock the next morning. He awoke in a cheerful mood and ate a hearty breakfast complete with "quite a number of little delicacies" – normal concessions to a condemned man.

As the time drew nearer, Smith showed great curiosity about the mechanics of the execution. He was especially curious whether he would be allowed to see his coffin. He asked one of the jailers, George Ritenour, why he would have to wear a black hood – was it to prevent his seeing his own execution? Ritenour wasted no tact, but explained that this was done to spare onlookers the ghastly distortions of a hanged man's face. In his usual matter-of-fact way, Smith observed that "this was certainly right."

When prison doctor E.H. Wynn came to his cell, "Smith's face lighted up in expectancy," and he asked for a detailed description of the sensations he could expect when the trap was sprung. He wondered how long it would likely take him to die, and whether he would be conscious to the last. Doctor Wynn assured him that the process was nearly painless, and Smith "seemed gratified." He said he had heard that such was the case, though one wonders from whom he'd heard it.

Smith was offered a cigar, which he passed on to Garbutt, claiming, "that was a habit he had never indulged in" – never mind that he'd bought several cigars the day he killed Isbell. At 9 a.m. Garbutt helped his cellmate dress in the outfit he had chosen to die in: a dark blue suit and a white shirt with turned-down collar. "When at 10 o'clock he was fully attired," gushed the *Dallas News*, "George Smith was decidedly a handsome man."

Smith refused the hordes of visitors – mainly curiosity seekers – who came to the jail hoping to speak with a man of his dubious celebrity. He had been "worried and irritated yesterday at so many," that today he made but few exceptions. He consented to see his "spiritual advisor," the Reverend George Gibbs of St. Stephen's Episcopal Church, who came accompanied by Mrs. Wright, a local woman who worked in prison ministry. Mrs. Wright stayed only a few minutes, but when she left Smith had "traces of tears in his eyes." Gibbs remained for three hours, talking to Smith of "the future and the certainties of a life beyond the grave." Smith told Gibbs he believed "that his nature had undergone a complete reformation and that he did not fear what might come after death."

Speaking of Smith's "calm demeanor when talking about his approaching doom," the *Dallas News* offered, "there is nothing but modesty. Smith has nothing of the bravo [sic] in his make-up." If only he had been so modest in January 1891.

Just after noon, Smith finished "a hearty meal." After lunch he received another clergyman, Reverend Bone of the Cumberland Presbyterian Church. After a "cheering consultation" Bone departed, leaving Reverend Gibbs and Smith alone from 1 p.m. to 2 p.m., during which Gibbs "continued in spiritual comfort."

Meanwhile, outside the death cell, Sheriff McAfee and jailer McKinney were seeing to final preparations for the hanging. "The catch on the trap door," the *Dallas News* reported, "had been fixed to avoid any catch or hitch. The iron brace and ring to which the rope was fastened had been tested by an adequate weight, and everything was in readiness long before the time. The rope was in readiness to be placed around the prisoner's neck." Back in his cell George Smith readied that neck by bowing it with Gibbs in a final prayer.

Just after 2 p.m. Doctors Wynn and King came to the cell and injected Smith with a quarter gram of morphine. Shortly after this Smith was visited by a final clergyman vying for his soul: Dr. T. J. Simmons of the Methodist Episcopal Church. Waiting in the jail's rotunda were the various officials and the witnesses who would observe Smith's execution. Along with reporters from nearly every Grayson County newspaper, there were prison officials, deputy sheriffs, justices of the peace, "the six freeholders" (county commissioners) plus "five friends of Smith." The accounts don't specify how many of those friends may have been clergy.

At 2:18 sharp, McAfee and several reporters entered Smith's cell for the last formality – the reading of the death warrant. Smith stood this ritual at first with his customary stoicism; he "answered the sheriff with a firm 'All right, sir.'" He stood with hands clasped behind him while McAfee read, some nervousness now betrayed by his shifting feet, restless eyes and twitching mouth. Still, the ever-admiring *Dallas News* declared that "he was meeting his fate with a wonderful fortitude." As the reading concluded Smith paced a bit and mopped his brow, but afterward he seemed to rally and become even more determined to display a calm resolve.

At 2:23, with a "firm step" Smith walked with the sheriff to the gallows. He wore a yellow rose in his lapel, and his natty shirt collar had been removed to facilitate the noose. At McAfee's direction, Smith stepped upon the trap door and turned to face east. As the deputies bound his legs, he "looked at them intently," and as they prepared to bind his hands behind him he asked, "Wouldn't you just as soon tie them in front of me?" The men explained they were required to fasten his hands in back, so Smith asked that they "be pinioned more securely, which was granted."

As the Sheriff prepared to place the black hood over his head, Smith looked at Rev. Gibbs, who stood nearby and said, "Good-by, Mr. Gibbs."

"Then the black mask came down," wrote the *Dallas News*, "and George Smith had looked for the last time on earth." He'd never see the coffin propped on two chairs beneath the trap. But Smith couldn't resist a last-minute bit of carping. "A fellow can't breathe much in this," he groused. As McAfee dropped the noose over his head and snugged the knot down, Smith said, "That is pretty tight." The complaint, and the words, were his last.

"At 2:28 p.m.," the *Dallas News* reported, "the trap was sprung and the body shot with rapidity through the open door." It was a clean death, as hangings go, "with none of the terrible twisting and writhings which usually sicken spectators."

For all his death cell posturing and confabs with clergy over his eternal fate, there is no record that George Smith ever spoke a single word of contrition over Jim Isbell's death, or made any expression of sympathy whatsoever for the loved ones Isbell left behind. Shortly before his hanging, Smith complained to jailers when he learned he'd be led to the gallows in his stocking feet, saying he had "supposed they would have let him die with his boots on." The irony was lost on him that James F. Isbell would no doubt have preferred to die *sans* boots, but that Smith had stolen that chance forever.

Chapter 6: *"They posed as young men of leisure, with a fad for bicycle riding."*
Sheriff John Jasper Bogard
Tehama County, California (March 30, 1895)

What is it this time? This was probably the first thing passengers on Oregon Express No. 15 thought as the train came to a stop in the moonless night. It was 1:45 a.m. and the train, bound from Sacramento to Portland, was less than a quarter mile short of its next stop, Reed's Station, seven miles south of Marysville, California. The train had been delayed over an hour just outside of Sacramento the evening before due to an overheated axle bearing. Maybe the repairs hadn't fixed the problem.

Riders in the day coach had their questions answered as the forward door jerked open and four men strode through. Two they recognized as trainmen: the engineer, Amos Bowsher, and his fireman, Barney Nethercott. The others were strangers – a tall, lanky fellow with a no-nonsense air and a short, nervous man with a roosterish swagger. The cloth masks covering their faces and the pistols in their fists, however, left no doubt as to why the train had stopped.

The bandits relieved about half a dozen passengers of their goods and had just crossed into the smoking car when the door at the car's other end swung open and a lone man came quickly through, pistol in hand. The trainmen recognized him, as several of the passengers likely did. Others no doubt thought him another holdup man, at least until he ducked behind the seats on one side of the aisle, leveled his gun, and with a single shot toppled the tall, grim robber into the aisle. In an instant the car was filled with deafening gunfire and smoke so dense it snuffed out the wall-mounted lanterns. When the noise and gun smoke had subsided, the lamps were relit. The short, strutting bandit had fled, and a dead man lay at either end of the car. One was a career train robber whose identity would be clinched by the mode of transportation he'd chosen for his planned getaway. The other was Sheriff John Jasper Bogard.

A native of Chillicothe, Missouri, John Bogard was born June 22, 1851. He'd come to California as a boy and for many years worked as a farmer and sheep rancher in Tehama County. He married Anna Louise Gibbs in Tehama just five days short of his 28th birthday. The couple would have three children: Della, born in 1880; Eleanor, born in 1881; and George, born in 1884.

Bogard was first elected sheriff of Tehama County in 1892. He proved to be so successful and popular that in 1894 he won reelection "by a handsome majority." In his brief career as a lawman, Bogard had quickly become known as "a terror to evildoers," with unusually great detective skills owing in part to a photographic memory for faces. He was also a man who "displayed a recklessness and daring in times of danger that surprised his friends." Milton Sharp, the "Gentleman

Sheriff John J. Bogard was known for his memory for faces and his dogged determination, both handy attributes for a lawman. *(Photo courtesy of Jeanne Ware Henry and Richard L. Henry – great granddaughter and great-great grandson of John J. Bogard)*

Bandit" who'd robbed stage coaches in California and Nevada throughout the 1880s, witnessed firsthand Bogard's daring and acumen in October 1893.

Sharp had escaped from the Nevada State Prison in Carson City in 1889 and had been on the run ever since. When he made the blunder of going into Red Bluff, Sheriff Bogard collared the notorious highwayman as easily as if he'd been the town drunk, and Sharp quickly found himself back in the Nevada pen.

On March 30, 1895, Bogard was aboard the Oregon Express on business, following up a lead in a Yolo County train robbery from several months prior. He was sleeping in a Pullman car when the train stopped at Wheatland to take on water, and unbeknownst to Bogard or anyone else, two masked men slipped aboard before the train continued on. About half a mile out from Wheatland the bandits climbed from a boxcar onto the locomotive's tender and from there jumped into the cab. As Bowsher later described it, "someone punched me quite forcibly in the ribs and I turned around to see that it was a masked man, a tall fellow with two pistols, which he held uncomfortably close to me. Behind my fireman, I noticed another man, a shorter one, also masked and armed similarly. I said to the tall man, 'Hello, what do you want?' He replied, 'We want you to stop at the next crossing.'"

As they neared a crossroad, the tall robber ordered Bowsher to brake. When the train had stopped, the robbers forced Bowsher and Nethercott to jump from the cab, then made the men accompany them to the express car. The tall robber had Bowsher shout a warning to Forest Kelton, the Wells Fargo messenger inside, that the robbers would dynamite the car if he didn't open up post haste. Kelton slid open the door, the bandits ordered him out, and the tall robber climbed into the car while his partner remained on guard outside. The man searched the car in vain. All the valuables were locked in the through safe, and Wells Fargo had recently adopted the policy – due to a rash of robberies – of not giving its express messengers the combinations to through safes. Since the dynamite was a bluff and they had no way to open the safe, the robber took only Kelton's express company shotgun, which he handed out to his partner saying, "Here is a bouquet for you, Bill." ("Bill," it turned out, was their shared code name.)

The gunmen were not happy at being unable to loot the express car. "This made the fellows so hot," Nethercott recalled, "that they said they would take on the whole train, and they went right at it." As they marched the trainmen toward the passenger cars, one of them handed Nethercott a makeshift loot sack formed from the ragged leg of a pair of overalls knotted at one end. Preceded by Nethercott and Bowsher, the robbers mounted the platform and entered the day coach. At the tall man's command all hands went up. The party made its way down the aisle, Nethercott leading the way. Prodded by the robbers' pistols, he held out the sack to receive passengers' money, watches, and other valuables as the tall robber gruffly ordered them to "Dig up." When a passenger named Sampson refused to hand over his goods, the tall robber gave him a savage pistol-whipping, inflicting a four-inch gash in his scalp. Mr. Samson grudgingly complied.

As the robbers entered the day coach the train's brakeman, George Summers, realized what was taking place. He knew Bogard was aboard and sent a porter to summon him. The porter hurried to the sleeper and awoke Bogard, who threw on his trousers and overcoat, grabbed his pistol, and headed toward the coaches. He'd have to face the threat alone; though armed guards had been riding the line recently due to a spate of holdups, the Southern Pacific had halted the practice only two days earlier.

The bandits and their reluctant assistants moved on to the smoking car. They shouted another hands-up order which so surprised the passengers that as they raised their hands some "held their lighted cigars between their fingers." Just as they entered through the forward door and were stripping the first passenger of valuables, Bogard sidled in through the rear door and took what cover he could between seats.

Sheriff Bogard carried his Merwin, Hulbert revolver in a "Bridgeport rig" – a patented, holsterless design that secured the weapon via a stud attached to its frame to a special spring-steel clip on the belt, thus allowing quick access. The rig shown here is a replica; the pistol is Sheriff Bogard's. (*Photo courtesy of Richard L. Henry – great-great grandson of John J. Bogard*)

Eyewitness accounts, no doubt affected by adrenaline, dense black powder smoke, and blinding and deafening muzzle blasts, vary as to exactly what took place next. Bowsher was near enough, he later testified, that Bogard could whisper, "How many?" and the engineer could offer a sotto voce "Two."

Acting quickly, Bogard took aim and shot the tall robber, who fell with a bullet hole in his chest. Kelton was standing between the shorter robber and Bogard; as the sheriff changed positions to have a clear shot, the masked man opened fire. Bogard dropped instantly, shot in the small of the back. "The wound must have been immediately fatal," the *San Francisco Call* reported, "for the Sheriff dropped to his knees and sank to the floor between the box and the stove. He made no sound or motion after that, and was doubtless dead before he struck the floor."

Dying from his wound, the downed robber fired blindly with his own pistols, managing only to shoot Nethercott in the shoulder and leg. "I am done for!" he cried, as his partner came to his side and asked, "Are you killed, Bill?" The wounded man pleaded, "Don't leave me, Bill. Take me with you." The shorter robber apparently recognized that his partner was as good as dead; without even bothering to take the bag of loot he "ran out of the door and escaped in the darkness."

Nethercott staggered into the day coach still clutching the robbers' sack, which held half a dozen watches, several purses, and "a considerable amount of gold and silver coin and currency." He told the porter, "I am shot all to pieces," and handed him the sack.

Back in the smoker, the trainmen re-lighted the lamps and took stock of the situation. Bogard was dead, as was the tall robber. When they pulled off his mask they found he was wearing a false beard, held on by two strings tied at the top of his head. He was dressed in a sweater and overalls, the pockets of which were lined with heavy toweling, creating makeshift holsters for his two Colt revolvers. Most interestingly, under his outer clothing he wore a full "bicycle suit" – short jacket, knickers with long black stockings, and a jaunty, short-billed cap – a trendy garment of the day favored by recreational bicyclists. This attire would soon help the authorities put names to the dead robber and his pal.

Shortlidge tapped a passenger to act as fireman in the injured Nethercott's place, and the train was soon underway again, arriving in Marysville around 2:30 a.m. They had telegraphed ahead from Reed's Station and were met at the Marysville depot by Police Officer Meek, who took custody of the abandoned loot and the dead men's sidearms. Bogard's Merwin-Hulbert revolver held two expended rounds and another with a dented primer, an obvious misfire. One of the bandit's pistols held three spent cartridges.

Marysville doctor David Powell was summoned to the train station, where he took charge of the wounded fireman. One of the robber's bullets had entered Nethercott's right shoulder and torn across his back to lodge in his left shoulder. Another went through the back of his left leg and stopped just above his knee. Dr. Powell treated the wounds and had the patient transferred to the southbound train for transport back to Sacramento. Coroner Richard Bevan arrived shortly after Dr. Powell and examined the dead. He found that the sheriff's marksmanship had been superb; his bullet had gone completely through the dead robber's body, piercing the heart. Sheriff Bogard had been struck by a single round in the main right artery, just below his kidneys.

Telegrams immediately went out throughout the region alerting lawmen that Bogard had been murdered and that his killer was on the loose. Response was quick; Placer County Sheriff William Conroy, an old friend and colleague who had ridden many a trail with Bogard, left Auburn at 4 a.m. By 5 a.m., news had reached Sheriff Sam Inlow of Yuba County, and he headed for Marysville. As word spread, a virtual who's-who of California's best known lawmen poured into the area to help. Though "mutual aid" agreements were not formalized as they are today, sheriffs from neighboring counties responded to the hue and cry. Tom Cunningham (San Joaquin County), Frank T. Johnson (Sacramento County), Tom Houston (Shasta County) all answered the call, while Tehama County was represented by undersheriff Andrew Jackson "Jack" Bogard, John Bogard's brother, who would soon be appointed to the late sheriff's post.

These public officers were joined by private lawmen with equally impressive reputations. James B. Hume was Wells Fargo's detective par excellence; he and his right hand man, Jonathan Thacker, were a plague to California's stagecoach and train robbers. The Southern

Pacific Railroad was well-represented by its chief detective, George Gard, a career lawman who'd served as the Chief of Police in Los Angeles, as Los Angeles County Sheriff, and as a United States Marshal during his career.

Rounding out the able team of lawmen was the San Francisco Police Department's chief of detectives, Captain Isaiah Lees, one of the Golden State's most formidable manhunters. By 7 a.m. a special train from San Francisco to Marysville carried an army of deputies and detectives, and newspapers expressed "no doubt that the remaining desperados would be captured." There would be no shortage of assistance; the killing of a lawman was, and is, a personal affair to other officers. "It would be almost impossible," reported the *San Francisco Call* the next day, "to gather together a more disgusted assortment of detectives, sheriffs and officers than can be found in Sacramento to-night."

Within hours after word of Bogard's death went out, posses were scouring the scene of the robbery and the surrounding countryside and towns, searching for his killer, while detectives began following up on all available clues. By the time most of these officers took to the trail, they already knew whom they were hunting, if not his true name. A couple of Marysville hotel clerks had viewed the dead robber's body and identified him as one Sam McGuire, a gent who'd arrived in town on March 25, claiming to be a bicycle agent from San Francisco. McGuire had been in the company of a shorter fellow with a "small, sandy mustache," and a "swagger walk." The tall man had registered at the Golden Eagle Hotel as "S. McGuire." His friend had registered at the United States Hotel as "J. Johnson," but had also given his name about town as "G. Williams." Both had been in possession of bicycles, and both had been seen leaving town, heading south on their "wheels" at about 10 p.m. the night of March 29.

Initial reports, based on the location of Bogard's wound and spurious news dispatches detailing "eyewitness accounts," led the lawmen to believe at first that a third robber had shot Sheriff Bogard from behind. As they developed the case and evidence mounted, they discarded the "third robber" scenario and focused efforts on tracking down the short bandit.

The following day, Sacramento County Sheriff Johnson received a message from the home of Daniel Ostrom, a former Yuba County assemblyman who owned a farm at Reed's Crossing. Ostrom's sons, T.J. and George, had found a bicycle stashed underneath a railroad bridge about a mile north of the holdup site. Two sets of bicycle tracks where the wheel was found convinced the lawmen that they were on the right trail. The robbers had likely secreted their bicycles here and walked the six miles to Wheatland. It seemed the fugitive robber was still on his wheel, or had left the scene on it at any rate.

The bicycles were a promising lead in more than Sheriff Bogard's murder. Lees was doubly interested in the case, for there were similarities between it and a San Francisco murder two weeks earlier. On March 16, two masked men had entered the Ingleside House Saloon and robbed it at gunpoint. When the proprietor, Cornelius Stagg, resisted, the taller of the two bandits shot and killed him. The robbers fled with a paltry four dollars and seemingly vanished into mist; no horses or wagons were seen leaving the area. It was well known that a two-man team had carried out the crime – a tall, bold man and a short, jumpy fellow. But the cagey Lees had held some key facts back from the press. One of these was that an officer searching the area had found footprints; another was that they found bicycle tracks. Lees was too shrewd a detective to put much store in coincidence. He was convinced from the outset that the Oregon Express robbers were his bicycle bandits as well. And the same duo, it appeared, may have been responsible for a string of similar saloon robberies and several other train holdups stretching back several months.

The bicycle found by the Ostrom boys bore the name of a wheel shop in San Francisco. A representative dispatched to Marysville identified the dead robber as a customer, known to him as Sam McGuire, who had purchased the bicycle in October 1894. The representative, J.W. Leavitt, said McGuire had returned to the shop on March 11 and rented a similar model, which he returned on the 18th, two days after the Stagg murder. At that time Leavitt had noticed fresh scratches on McGuire's face, which he claimed came from taking "a header" on the bicycle. Lees had also withheld from the public evidence that while fleeing their crime the Ingleside robbers had run headlong into a barbed-wire fence.

Following a lead developed by the Southern Pacific men on the case, Lees and a team of detectives, including Gard, visited a home at 305 Grove Street in San Francisco where, if their information was correct, "Williams," alias "Johnson," alias "Jack McGuire" roomed. The tip proved correct, except that here the polynymous fugitive was known by yet another name, Jack Brady. Johanna Liljequist, the landlady, gave the detectives access to Brady's room and inside they found, literally, a treasure chest. A trunk with markings indicating it belonged to Henry "Harry" Williams contained a large number of photographs, including two tintypes showing a pair of men nattily attired in bicycle suits, astride their wheels. The taller of the two was their dead robber; the landlady identified the shorter one as Jack Brady.

Brady had roomed at the house since early November. According to Mrs. Liljequist and her daughter Tillie, he was a quiet, well-behaved sort who "went to bed at very good hours" and "neither smoked, chewed nor drank." Mrs. Liljequist told Lees that Williams/Brady had occasionally been away overnight, claiming that his work required travel. She informed Lees that Brady's only visitor – and a frequent one – during his residence there, was a tall gent named McGuire. The description perfectly fit the dead Oregon Express robber.

Tillie Liljequist seemed more than casually interested in their lodger. Though Gard learned there had been "some trouble" between

Brady and the landlady's daughter and "they did not speak to each other for two months." Miss Liljequist told Gard that despite the standing reward of $50,000 offered for Brady's capture, she would not inform against him. Though the clearly-smitten girl wasn't about to peach, she did offer up one tantalizing tidbit. Some months earlier, she told Gard, she had accepted Brady's offer to go for a bicycle ride. At some point their conversation turned to robberies, and Brady said that if he were a robber and should ever be cornered by the law, "he would kill himself rather than be captured."

This was as much as the Liljequist ladies would offer. When Lees asked consent to occupy Brady's room and lie in wait for his return – offering to pay rent – the ladies flatly refused and the captain "had to be satisfied with the thought that he could leave a couple of his men to shadow the house."

From the Liljequist home, Lees and his team went to a house at 626 Golden Gate, where they had information the dead robber, whom they now believed to be named Sam Browning, had lodged. The residents there "were horrified when they were informed of the identity of their former lodger."

When Gard described the late bandit and his fugitive friend, "they were satisfied that it was Browning or Maguire [sic] as they knew him and his only visitor, Brady."

In Browning's room, the officers found a trunk the same make as Brady's, but larger. This, too, was a bonanza; in it Lees found pictures galore of the dead robber and his pal (including more of Browning and Brady in bike garb), muddy shoes (size 9 ½, which matched prints left by Stagg's killer) and a number of pawn tickets, one of which was for a "Cleveland wheel" pawned by Brady (as "McGuire") on January 31. In the tintypes of the two men in bicycle suits, each was wearing a short-billed bicycle cap – the same sort the dead Browning wore.

To aid the hunt for Jack Brady, the *San Francisco Chronicle* published this sketch of the "bicycle bandits," done from one of the photographs Captain Lees found in Browning's and Brady's effects. *(Author's Collection)*

Eyewitnesses at the Ingleside House holdup had described the bandits as wearing similar caps. Long mackintosh coats found in each man's trunk likewise fitted descriptions of the robbers' attire in several recent holdups; Lees theorized that the coats had been worn to conceal bicycle suits.

As the various agencies pursuing Brady compared notes, they formed the opinion that Browning and Brady were their men in more than just the Bogard and Stagg cases. A string of robberies throughout the region stretching back for many months had much in common. All featured a pair of bandits – a tall, lanky, aggressive sort who did all the talking, and a small, stoop-shouldered, quiet fellow who walked with a cocksure strut, but whose trembling hands betrayed his nervousness.

Along with the physical evidence, Lees and the other lawmen began to establish a solid timeline. The respective landlords confirmed overnight absences for both men that matched the dates of several robberies. In October, each had paid cash for a Cleveland bicycle from the Frisco shop; Brady had pawned his on January 31, and Browning's was the one found by the Ostroms. On March 11, Browning had rented another bicycle from manager Leavitt, saying that he and Brady were going for "a ride in the country." Browning returned the bicycle two days after the Stagg murder.

The noose was tightening figuratively – and possibly soon literally – around the errant Brady's neck. Though witnesses said the taller robber had shot Stagg, reports were confused as to which bandit had shot Bogard. But who had pulled the trigger was beside the point. California law at the time – as it does today – included a "felony murder" rule; anyone participating in a specified felony crime, robbery among them, could be prosecuted for first degree murder if a death resulted. If caught, Brady was apt to hang.

Despite Lees having his men watch the Liljequist house, there was no sign of Brady's attempting to return home. The manhunt dragged on for weeks. Tips came in frequently; "Brady" was seen riding a ferry here, hopping a train there, stopping at a remote farmhouse to cadge a meal. Officers combed the area chasing these leads and taking a hard look, of course, at anyone traveling by bicycle. It was a bad time to be a bike enthusiast in California; anyone astride a wheel was suspect.

Complicating the search was the presence of a number of ad hoc bounty hunters and would-be sleuths. "The large reward offered for the capture of the missing desperado," wrote the *San Francisco Chronicle*, "has brought out hundreds of wild-eyed amateur detectives and a good wind storm would fill the streets with unshorn men and the air with false beards. A bicyclist with gold in his front teeth should keep off the roads of Yuba, Sutter and Tehama Counties. Nothing but the jail waits a wheelman of this description."

As investigators identified the robbers, and their descriptions and other information was disseminated via official channels and published in newspapers, detectives were flooded with tips – some good, most useless. The majority of the reported sightings proved to be, as the *Los Angeles Times* put it, "wind and nothing more." Though accounts varied in some details, the robbers were identified as follows: The dead robber was one S.O. (possibly Samuel Oscar) Browning, alias Oscar Brown, of Missouri. He was about 22 years old, stood a little over six feet tall, weighed 200 to 230 pounds, and had a dark complexion, dark hair and a small moustache. When killed, he was wearing a "complete bicycle suit" under a pair of overalls and was armed with two Colt revolvers, one of which had been taken from the Wells Fargo messenger in a March 8 train robbery, north of Stockton.

The fugitive robber was identified as Henry (or Harry) Williams, alias Jack (or John) Brady, born in Illinois. He was about 33 years old, about five-foot-seven, 120-125 pounds, with a light complexion, light hair and a sandy moustache. Gold-capped teeth flanked his front two uppers. He had a round-shouldered build and a fidgety manner.

He had been carrying a revolver and a short-barreled shotgun, the latter of which he'd dropped when he fled the Oregon Express.

The two bandits' history together went back three years at least; they were believed to have met on a boat to Stockton in early 1892. Later that year both worked for a rancher in Amador County, but not for long. They stole four horses from their employer and made for San Francisco, where police arrested them as they tried to sell the animals. Tried and convicted for horse theft as Henry Williams and Oscar Brown, each was sentenced to a year in San Quentin prison. A character reference from a prior employer of Brady's may have helped buy lighter sentences; in any case, prisoners #15023 (Brady) and #15027 (Browning) were discharged from San Quentin on May 11, 1893.

They didn't walk the straight and narrow for long; they were implicated in a saloon robbery in Sacramento in August 1894, and a similar robbery at Scheld's Brewery just a few nights later. They robbed the Cliff House Saloon in San Francisco on September 25, and shot proprietor Robert Hagerty. Their big take came on October 12 when they robbed the Omaha Overland Train near Davisville and netted $53,000. In the later part of October, they robbed a saloon "near the City and County Hospital" in Sacramento. In late February 1895, they again struck the Cliff House Saloon, robbing Frank Hagerty, Robert's brother, and four customers. In the early hours of March 3, two men of like description held up an eastbound train at Ben Ali, but got away with no money or valuables. The same night they paid a second visit to Scheld's, robbing several card players and making off with thirteen dollars from the till. On March 8, the men again stopped the eastbound train, this time three to four miles north of Stockton. Once more, they got no money, but relieved the express messenger of his pistol and shotgun.

Brady's pursuers were pleased to be closing the net on Bogard's killer; solving so many other cases was a welcome bonus. "We are perfectly satisfied," Gard told the *San Francisco Call*, "that the same two men committed all these robberies. Their height, costume (as you may call it) and build, and the manner in which they acted, all agree perfectly. The tall man was always the aggressor, and there are other coincidences that satisfy us on the point."

Sheriff Cunningham had come to San Francisco on March 19, trailing the Ben Ali robbers and had joined in the search for Stagg's killers, whom he believed to be the same men. If not for the zeal of the local press, he might have caught his men and unwittingly saved Sheriff Bogard's life. "He was very much chagrined," wrote the *Call* without apology, "when the object of his visit was published, and bluntly said that there was no use of looking longer for them here, as they would have left the city."

"There was a feeling of relief at police headquarters yesterday," the *Call* reported, "when it was proved beyond doubt...that the two men who held up the Oregon Express at Reed's Crossing, near Marysville, were the same two men who committed the robbery and murder at the Ingleside House on March 16 and various other robberies in and outside the city."

This jubilation faded somewhat as the onerous task of tracking their man wore on and weeks turned into months. The officers feared that Brady was hiding on a large plot of land known as the Haggin Grant, or El Rancho Del Paso, a vast area of a hundred square miles bordered by the American and Sacramento Rivers. "On this immense body of land," claimed the *Call*, "a man could secret himself for months without enduring any privation, save that of solitude." The area was a fugitive's paradise, with herds of sheep and cattle, farm houses whose gardens could be pilfered, plenty of water and, best of all, plenty of hiding places. "It is an absolute impossibility," the paper went on, "to capture any person in this vast tract of brush-covered country, filled as it is with old mining shafts and drifts, without enlisting the services of an army of men and carefully scrutinizing every foot of the ground."

Officers combed the area as best they could and continued to run down reported sightings on the Haggin Grant and elsewhere. The last confirmed Brady sighting had been the day after Bogard's murder, when he'd been seen near the Twelfth Street bridge leading into Sacramento, his presence later confirmed by shoe prints in the mud. A lucky break came in mid-June when a constable at Cottonwood, near Redding, passed a man driving a horse and cart on the road at the outskirts of town. The constable, George Martin, was carrying a picture of Brady and recognized him at once.

Martin hustled back into town for backup and returned in a cart with a man named Mart Bowers. The men followed Brady's tracks north to a bridge at Clear Creek. Here the tracks petered out, but as the two crossed the bridge Bowers spotted Brady's rig tied up creekside about a hundred yards upstream. Brady was nowhere in sight. As Martin and Bowers drew near, Brady popped up from the other side of a grassy embankment, brandishing a shotgun. Martin raised his own scattergun and cut loose, knocking the bandit down. Brady fired as he fell, his charge narrowly missing Martin's head. Bowers jumped down and he and Brady began trading fire with only Martin's horse between them. One of Brady's shots hit Bowers' hand, nearly clipping off a fingertip, but not before the posseman wounded him again.

Both Brady's and Martin's horses were injured in the fracas. Brady abandoned his stolen horse and cart while Martin's horse panicked and ran off, smashing its driverless rig to pieces in the flight. Afoot and out of ammunition, Martin and Bowers retreated into town, and a posse was soon in the field. Reports were optimistic; an Associated Press dispatch from Cottonwood claimed that "the bandit is surrounded, and it is only the question of a few hours when he will be captured or killed."

Such reports proved to be premature, however. By nightfall, Brady was still at large. "It is thought," said the *San Francisco Call*, that Brady "was mortally wounded and will be found laying dead along the creek somewhere when the search is resumed at daylight."

But Brady's outlaw luck held. He was still very much alive. There were sightings – that evening he'd been seen leaning against a rock and dripping blood not far from the shootout scene. A few days later a man of his description wearing a brown eye patch oozing blood begged supper at a house between Cottonwood and Ball's Ferry. Still, it seemed only a matter of time now, and if Brady were truly lucky, it would be lawmen who brought him in. The Cottonwood fight had ignited a smoldering vigilante fever among the local populace. A private letter to Sacramento from Redding reported citizens were "fully determined to lynch the bandit," and that if captured the night of the fight, "he would have been strung up to the nearest telegraph pole." If Brady had been in earnest when he talked suicide to Tillie Liljequist, it seemed that to make good he only needed to surrender to a civilian posse.

But Brady wasn't cornered just yet. He may even have struck back; the barn at Constable Martin's home in Cottonwood was mysteriously burned less than a week after their skirmish. For a month after his narrow escape, Brady continued to elude posses, and sightings were once again reported all over the region. On July 23, Sheriff Johnson was combing the Haggin Grant with bloodhounds when he received reports of a heavily armed man of Brady's description seen skulking through the nearby brush on horseback. Johnson and several deputies tracked the man and found that he'd abandoned his hard-ridden horse, stashed his saddle in the brush, and caught a ferry across the river fifteen miles above Sacramento. The ferry operator recognized a photo of Brady and said he had been "very excited and kept looking back" during the crossing and had taken to the brush when they landed, heading southwest toward Woodland. News reports predicted that Johnson's group of "experienced and gamey [sic] officers" would soon give Brady "a battle which will not resemble the burlesque skirmish which recently took place in Shasta County." It was easy for reporters to take written potshots at the Cottonwood men; they hadn't been there swapping real lead with Jack Brady.

The next day's reports had Brady both in Swingles Station, eight miles west of Sacramento, and also several miles north of Ukiah. The Ukiah report was more promising; Brady had been identified by a rancher near Lakeport who'd let a stranger stop for the night and had given him directions to Humboldt County. The rancher described the man as "injured in the right leg and wounded in the left eye and armed with two revolvers."

The following day, July 25, the long manhunt came to an abrupt end. After four months on the run, the wily bicycle bandit was betrayed at last – not by confederates or informants, but by his own stomach. Having subsisted for days on nothing but purloined peaches, Brady risked a quick trip into the little town of Freeport, just ten miles south of Sacramento, where he went into a small grocery store to buy some crackers and canned oysters. The storekeeper, Phil Riehl, noticed that his customer seemed engrossed in, and disturbed by, a newspaper he'd picked up from the counter. When the stranger hurried from the store, Riehl examined the newspaper and saw a prominent piece detailing the local hunt for bandit Brady. The description clicked, and Riehl immediately telephoned the Sacramento County Sheriff's office.

Deputies hurried to Riehl's store and began an intense area search. Early the next morning, Deputy Sheriff Alexander McDonald and Richland Justice of the Peace William Johnson, part of the search team, were passing through a rural area between Richland and Courtland, about twenty miles south of Sacramento, when they spotted a short man sitting under a bridge. As they quietly moved closer, they recognized Brady.

Before Brady could react, the men threw down on him and ordered him to surrender. The bold-talking, never-be-taken-alive bandit offered not a whit of resistance, but very meekly submitted to arrest. He denied that he was Brady, of course, but the officers were carrying his photograph. A bundle in his possession contained a short-barreled shotgun which later proved to be the Wells Fargo weapon taken in the March 8 holdup. After 118 days on the run, Jack Brady was in custody and on his way to jail in Sacramento.

News of Brady's capture spread like wildfire and "naturally created quite a sensation in Sacramento," said the *Los Angeles Times.* "Throngs of curious people were in and out of Sheriff Johnson's office all afternoon, hoping for a chance to see the notorious criminal." If they expected to see a crazed, wild-eyed boogeyman, they were disappointed. "Brady is an undersized man and has an

BANDIT JACK BRADY, DOOMED TO LIFE IMPRISONMENT FOR THE KILLING OF SHERIFF BOGARD.

The word "doomed" under this *San Francisco Call* sketch of Brady (also from a photograph found among the robbers' property) might have been better used to describe Sheriff Bogard's fate than his killer's. *(Author's Collection)*

effeminate voice," the *Times* groused. "He is far from the dime novel desperado. He looks so insignificant now that any man would not hesitate to meet him upon any sort of fighting proposition." For the bandit's part, he seemed to be enjoying his celebrity and "would have spun off yard after yard of stories about himself for he is considerable of a egotist." But Brady had little chance for yarn-spinning; as soon as Wells Fargo detective Thacker arrived at the jail, "he put a stop to any further free exhibition."

Brady denied any connection with the various crimes laid to him, especially the two hanging offences – the Oregon Express robbery and the Stagg killing. He admitted knowing Browning but claimed that he and the tall man argued and "fell out" a few days before the holdup. When Samson, the passenger cold-cocked on the Oregon Express, was brought in to confront him, Brady denied ever seeing the man before, calming asserting, "I was not on that train." If true, he was asked, why had he gone underground and resisted capture by the Cottonwood posse? "Because it looked like they had a dead case against me," he answered. He swore he had not intentionally fired on the posse, but that his gun misfired when he fell.

Though he denied involvement with any robbery, Brady agreed to accompany Sheriff Johnson to Yolo County and help locate the money from the October train robbery, claiming that Browning had told him where it was buried. Officers searched in vain for the loot; their man was either playing coy or honestly did not know where it was cached.

Brady became slightly more cooperative the following day when he was given into Sheriff's Inlow's custody for return to Marysville. He now confessed his part with Browning in the Davisville robbery, remarking how astounded the two were to discover that they had "captured a fortune of $53,000." He claimed they had held out but $1,600 and buried the rest. They went from there to San Francisco he said and "led a riotous life, spending their money on women and wine." Then, Brady insisted, despite several return trips to dig up the remainder of their booty, they were never able to locate it. For once, he was being honest. It would later turn out that a tramp, who by mere chance had seen the robbers burying their loot, had dug it up himself and was living like a railroad baron in San Francisco.

Brady remained in the county lockup at Marysville until his preliminary hearing before Justice Aldrich on August 12. Aldrich heard testimony from Bowsher and the other trainmen, plus testimony about the rented bicycle, the Ostroms' finding of the concealed bicycle, and from passengers who'd been held up on the train. Brady's defense counsel offered no testimony. Though the press covering the hearing lamented the prosecutor's "weak case," pointing out that the masks worn by the robbers prevented any positive identification of Brady, the defense voiced no opposition to the people's motion that he be held to answer. This was tactical; Sheriff Jack Bogard was said to be carrying a warrant in his pocket with intent to rearrest Brady if he were released. The lynch talk had reached Brady, and he feared for his neck if he were taken into Tehama County. Both the press and Brady fretted in vain; on August 13, Justice Aldrich ordered him held to answer for Bogard's murder and remanded him to Inlow's custody pending trial. On September 3, Brady pleaded "not guilty" at his arraignment before Superior Court Judge E.A. Davis at the Yuba County Courthouse. Judge Davis fixed a trial date of November 4.

When his day before the bar came at last, Brady made a good impression on at least some of the press covering the trial. The *Call* gushed, "'Gentleman Jack', as Brady is sometimes called, has none of the professional criminal about him. He is mild-mannered, pleasant, genial, and as fine a fellow as ever swung a revolver or robbed a train." Though Brady's true name was established early on as "Henry Williams" (to the court's satisfaction at least), the newspapers consistently used his alias. No doubt "Jack Brady" made for snappier headlines.

Jury selection took four days and the trial began in earnest on November 8. After opening statements, prosecutor Eugene McDaniel got down to business quickly, calling several witnesses who had been aboard the ill-fated Oregon Express. He would try right away to overcome his case's principal weakness: establishing that Brady was indeed the masked robber who shot and killed John Bogard. Though a passenger named Traynor thought Brady too tall to have been the bandit in question, two trainmen – engineer Bowsher and express messenger Kelton, expressed no doubt that Brady was the man. Bowsher was certain the smaller of the two robbers had shot the sheriff. "I know Bogard was hit," he testified, "because he lurched and fell against me, and would have fallen if I had not held him up."

Brady's lawyers, W.H. Carlin and E.A. Forbes of San Francisco, commenced pettifogging without delay. They questioned Bowsher's description of the short robber as "narrow-shouldered" and wasted much court time quibbling over the distinction between "stooped" and "round" shoulders; at the inquest, Bowsher had called the short robber's shoulders "stooped." The defense had Brady stand with his back to Bowsher and Judge Davis. "He looked," said the *Chronicle*, "like a Sandow" (Eugen Sandow was a well-known bodybuilder of the day). In his "new suit of clothes," wrote the *Call*, Brady's shoulders "appeared broad and square and his chest in general appearance that of a powerfully built young man."

Bowsher explained the discrepancy by pointing out that the man he'd seen shoot Bogard was "dressed differently." Attorney L.V. Hitchcock, hired by Jack Bogard to assist McDaniel, asked that Brady remove his coat. The difference was shocking. As the *Call* reported it, Brady's "stooped and rounded shoulders and narrow, contracted chest amounted to almost a deformity." Carlin's and Forbes' strategy had badly backfired. The only thing they'd proven to the jury was the skill of San Francisco tailors. "Bowsher's identification of the small robber," admitted the *Call*, "so far as the points were concerned, was completely justified." The case against Brady was looking stronger.

Testimony over the next couple of days dealt with establishing a link between Brady and Browning. If Brady couldn't positively be placed at the scene of Bogard's killing, the same was not true of his dead friend. Former companions of the pair, Marysville hotel clerks, and sundry merchants and other individuals who had encountered the men testified to their having been habitually in one another's company. The normally cocky Brady found this testimony worrisome. "He twists his moustache with evident vexation," reported the *San Francisco Chronicle*, "slides around in his chair or catches up a newspaper and pretends to read while he is biting his lips." Especially damning testimony came from Oroville merchant Max Marks, who had ridden the train with the two men from that city to Marysville days prior to the robbery. Marks detailed a lengthy conversation he'd had with Browning, who had claimed to be a bicycle repairman from San Francisco. According to Marks, Browning "asked a great number of questions about Reed's Station and the bridges," in particular the Yuba River bridge near Marysville.

Of course the cherry atop the prosecution's case was the tintype of the two bandits Captain Lees had found in Browning's trunk. It linked the two men, and showed their affinity for bicycling and bicycle attire. Lees himself appeared in court to verify this key piece of evidence and the other details his investigation had uncovered. The press still doubted the prosecution's case and proposed that Lees had a second motive for traveling to Marysville. The *Call* predicted Lees would "bring an important prisoner back with him – no less a prisoner, in fact, than the supposed murderer of Stagg at the Ingleside House last March." In the event of Brady's acquittal for the Bogard murder, the paper continued, Captain Lees intended to insure that Brady "does not have an opportunity to get back to his old haunts until the San Francisco courts are through with him." Prosecutors confirmed, meanwhile, that Jack Bogard held no warrant for Brady. While they bristled at the *Call*'s prediction of acquittal they admitted that, "you never know what twelve men are going to do." Its gloom-and-doom predictions aside, the *Call* ended the day's coverage on an optimistic note: "The chances are very favorable for Brady not outliving his old pal many more years."

It turned out the newspaper was mistaken on both counts, and the prosecution correct, both on its odds of conviction and the fickle nature of juries. Closing arguments began on November 15 and carried over to the 16th. Brady "shed tears" at Carlin's eloquence as the attorney claimed the prosecution's case was merely a "chain of rope and sand."

McDaniel's closing statement had only just begun when court adjourned for the day; as it was Saturday, he would wait until Monday the 18th to wrap up his arguments. That afternoon the jury went into deliberation, which was still in progress at midnight when Judge Davis ordered them sequestered for the night. When court reconvened at 9:30 a.m. on the 19th, there was still no verdict. When the noon hour passed with no change, the *San Francisco Call* reported that "the district attorney began to look serious and the lawyers for the defense complacent." Crowds loitered outside the courthouse anxiously awaiting the verdict, and the smart money was on acquittal.

At 5:05 p.m. the bailiff informed Judge Davis that the verdict was in. The court was reassembled, the jury filed in, and the curious poured inside and jockeyed for standing room. Judge Davis read the jury foreman's note with an impassive face and passed it to his clerk to read aloud. "Guilty as charged," announced the clerk.

Those not surprised at the verdict were almost certainly surprised at the sentence: life imprisonment. "11 Favored The Extreme Penalty, But Yielded To The 12th," read the headline in the *San Francisco Call*. The prolonged deliberations had been due to a single juror, later identified by the *Call* as San Francisco real estate man Sam Traynor. Though the finding of guilt was unanimous, he'd balked at sentencing Brady to hang.

Reports of Brady's reaction varied. The A.P. claimed he showed "a slight pallor" when the verdict was read, while the *Call* said he displayed no emotion but appeared to be "the calmest man in the room." A minor anticlimax was Judge Davis' citation of a spectator for contempt; he'd been overheard approaching a juror on November 14 and urging him to "hurry up and hang" Brady.

Judge Davis pronounced formal sentence on November 26. He refused Brady's request to be imprisoned at San Quentin rather than Folsom – an audacious appeal considering that just a day earlier Inlow's men had foiled Brady's attempt to break jail. Judge Davis countered with a list of reasons, starting with his belief "that Brady belonged to the worst criminal class, and is one of the most desperate of his class." He concluded with the opinion that "the defendant should feel exceedingly thankful that he is permitted to live anywhere upon earth." Brady was processed into Folsom prison forthwith.

The Marysville's stunt wouldn't be his last bid for freedom. On September 30 of the following year, Folsom's guards discovered an escape plan cooked up by Brady and his cellmate. Guards searching the men's cell found a handmade key that would unlock every cell on their block, and a blackjack fashioned from a length of rubber hose filled with lead. The guards removed the key, relocated the cell mate and kept close watch on Brady. Days later he was caught "red-handed" making another key.

Brady's name would come up several years later in connection with another prison break – this time for sitting it out. In July of 1903, several convicts broke out after killing a guard and taking the warden hostage. Prison officials learned later that the break's planners had intentionally left Brady out of the plot, because they didn't want any "notoriety" men along.

Brady had seemingly mellowed by 1913. Or at least his tactics had. In early September, newspapers carried reports of the onetime highwayman's midlife career change. "Once Train Robber has Turned Artist," proclaimed the *Fresno Morning Republican*. The *Oakland Tribune* announced "Train Robber is Now Sculptor." Having by his own account been something of an amateur sculptor in his youth, "before I ran wild and got into trouble," Brady had now given up the mask and revolver for the block and chisel. For the subject of his current piece he had chosen "no less a personage than Governor Hiram Johnson." If he were going to carve a portrait in stone, Brady must have reasoned, it may as well be of the man in charge of pardons. The work in question was a black marble medallion "about 12 inches in size" and "…surrounded by a frame carved from a solid piece of granite." The press highly praised "chiseller" Brady's artistry and workmanship. When finished, his project was shipped to Sacramento and presented to Johnson.

Whether Johnson was motivated by the impressive gift, his antipathy for the Southern Pacific (never mind that train robbery wasn't Brady's sole – or worst – crime), or his zeal for prison reform, shortly after his receipt of the sculpture Brady was paroled. On December 2, 1913, "Gentleman Jack" the erstwhile bicycle bandit, went free. Prison had taken its toll; the photo accompanying Brady's parole record shows a face looking twenty years older than its two-score-and-five or so years.

There were still those who remembered Sheriff Bogard, and who were outraged to hear of his killer breathing free air once more. An *Oakland Tribune* editorial on December 26, 1913, claimed Brady "was fortunate far behind his desserts when a chicken-hearted jury gave him a sentence of imprisonment instead of sending him to the gallows." The heinous crimes reported daily in the news, it went on, were "a bitter commentary on the misdirected clemency of the Prison Directors." Another editorial on December 30 fumed that Brady was "probably having a better time than many working men who never robbed or killed anyone."

A different take on Brady came from an ex-convict turned crime reformer named Jack Black. In his essay, "What's Wrong with the Right People?" in the June 1929 issue of *Harper's Magazine*, Black offered Brady as an example of his thesis that "the worst man is often the best bet" in terms of parole. "It is the petty criminal, the weak man, without character enough to be very good or very bad who violates parole or any sort of confidence." He claimed that "loyalty is the virtue of the underworld," and that an appeal to that loyalty was almost certain to produce a solid citizen. Even Sam Browning might have found that tough to swallow. His dying eyes had witnessed the extent of Jack Brady's loyalty.

Brady is said to have taken up ranching in his final years, with no evidence that his interest in sculpting extended beyond Governor Johnson's profile. The man who died and was buried at Humboldt as Thomas Henry Williams, on May 19, 1940, had led a colorful, misdirected, dime-novel life. Contrary to newspaper predictions of long past, he had outlived his fellow bicycle bandit – not to mention the stalwart sheriff of Tehama County – by just a few days short of forty-five years.

California Governor Hiram Johnson was a prison reformer, and no friend
of the Southern Pacific Railroad. Still, Jack Brady's prospects for a parole
were probably not hurt when the convict-artist sculpted the governor's image
in black marble and made him a gift of the piece. *(Photo courtesy of the Library
of Congress, Prints and Photographs Division)*

Chapter 7: *"They have done their duty and died for it, and no man can do more."*

Deputy Sheriff Daniel Carlyle Cameron
Deputy Sheriff Joseph John Lerri
Deputy Sheriff Charles Milton White
Deputy Sheriff George Clinton Woodsum
Constable Gustave Adolph Koch
Alameda County, California (July 19, 1898)

The concussion was felt as far away as San Jose, where residents naturally thought it was an earthquake. But it was no act of God. The great San Francisco earthquake was nearly eight years away, so the newspapers were probably justified in calling it "the most sensational tragedy every known in California." Arguably it still ranks as the Golden State's most sensational murder. Almost certainly it stands as the state's greatest loss of life to law enforcement in a single incident. Seven decades before the murders of four California Highway Patrol officers at Newhall, and over a century before Oakland itself lost four officers to a single gunman, five Alameda County officers fell in a deadly, surreal murder/suicide that began with – of all things – a lottery ticket.

In the summer of 1898, when much of it was far more sparsely settled than today, the rolling hills of Alameda County were home to a number of explosives plants. The combination of open spaces, easy railroad access, and nearby seaports made the area ideal for such industry. And business was thriving. Along with the normal commercial demands for dynamite and fuse used in construction and mining work, the discovery of gold in Alaska two years earlier and the rush for riches there had boosted the demand for explosives. The war with Spain had brought an ever increasing need for military ordnance.

One of the firms filling these needs was the Western Fuse and Explosives Company, located in Brooklyn Township, in Oakland's Melrose suburb (today's East Oakland). Built on Clark Street just east of High Street in 1888, the company shipped fifty million feet of fuse a year to customers around the world, all of it manufactured on-site and sent by the carload down the Southern Pacific tracks that lay just north of the works.

Most of the men who labored in the fuse works were Chinese immigrants hired, one supervisor explained, because they tended to be sober individuals who would not abandon their jobs at the first hint of a better offer. Sobriety was certainly a desired trait in men who worked with explosives, although the fact that the Chinese workers were paid a fraction of what white labor made must have made them all the more desirable.

One of these Chinese workers was a man on whose name history cannot seem to agree. Contemporary newspaper accounts and official records call him by a multitude of names, often within the same source. He is called Gung Wong Chang, Dong Ng Chang, Gong Ung Chung, Goon Ng Chung, Quong Chung, Quong Chank, and numerous other variations. The majority of sources seem to settle on Gung Ung Chang. Chang had been employed by the fuse works eight or nine years and was a reliable – if somewhat temperamental – worker whom the company superintendent considered "a careful man." As such, Chang was foreman of the "spinning room," the most dangerous area in the works, in which yarn was twisted around a gunpowder core to create fuse.

Though he may have been a sober and conscientious man on the job, Chang had a weakness for gambling, which was soon to be his undoing. A Chinese grocer from the city of Alameda made frequent meat and produce deliveries to the company and its workers, and did a brisk side business selling contraband Chinese lottery tickets. Like

Chang, the records call him by various names, the most frequent of which is Ham Si Sing. Though it violated state law, the lottery was a mania among the working class of Sing's countrymen; the previous year, the San Francisco Police Department reported confiscating twenty-six tons of the paper tickets. It was one such "seven-spot" ticket that brought about the bloody events of July 1898. Months earlier Sing had sold it to Chang, and the ticket had come up a winner, or Chang was convinced that it had. One account claims that it was Sing's cousin who'd sold Chang the ticket, and that he'd pocketed the winnings himself. Chang thought he was owed – accounts differ – $40 to $100, and each time the grocer visited the works Chang harangued him on the topic, to no avail.

In the early afternoon of July 18, Sing was making his usual deliveries and Chang was once more pressing him on the lottery winnings, with the usual result. The argument took place near a barracks-type building on the company grounds in which the Chinese workers were housed. This time Chang had had enough. Ducking into the workmen's quarters, he reappeared brandishing a hatchet. Before the fifty-seven-year-old Sing, who was seated, could defend himself, Chang launched a frenzied attack. His first blow fractured Sing's forehead and tore a nasty gash down the right side of his face, severing his ear. Another narrowly missed Sing's head but tore a sizable chunk out of his right shoulder. Sing fell to the ground stunned and bleeding, but Chang's fury wasn't yet spent. He ran back into the bunkhouse and emerged with a bulldog revolver in his fist. Standing over the wounded man, Chang pumped two bullets into Sing's body. The first slug tore into his abdomen; the second struck a pair of wire rimmed spectacles in his vest pocket and drove the nose piece into his body.

As his rage subsided and his head began to clear, the reality of what he had done came home to Chang. He must have known Sing was almost sure to die.

He must have realized that, no matter what his provocation, the law would see him as a murderer. He likely knew all too well what the white man's expression "a Chinaman's chance" meant. Whatever was in his head, Chang panicked. Still toting his hatchet and pistol, he headed for the one place he knew no one would dare come after him – the powder magazine.

The magazine, in one corner of the fuse works complex, was the storehouse where gunpowder was kept in twenty-five and fifty pound metal containers. Just how much and what type of powder was stored there – black powder or the more volatile and deadly giant powder – would later be a subject of fierce debate.

The magazine made an ideal makeshift fortress. It was built of brick, was about twenty feet square and ten feet

According to witnesses, Gung Ung Change used a bulldog pistol similar to this to kill Ham Si Sing, and possibly to touch off the explosion. *(Author's Collection)*

high, and had a sheet metal roof and a concrete floor a foot and half thick. It had only a single door, on the west, and a single grated window about fourteen by twenty inches on the east. It would do.

Occurring as it did in the middle of the workday, Chang's attack on Sing had not gone unnoticed. Other workers, including supervisors, were about the works and the plant was bordered on both Clark and High Streets with private homes – small frame cottages occupied by working class and struggling families. One of the neighbors was Charles Stephenson, a painter and a deputy constable for Brooklyn Township. Drawn by the sound of gunfire, Stephenson ran to the fuse works and found Ham Si Sing fearfully wounded but still alive. The Chinese laborers were already packing their scanty belongings and clearing out. They knew Gung Ung Chang too well to tarry.

Stephenson and "some white men" carried Sing to a nearby saloon – possibly George Giblin's place on High Street – and laid him out on a table. Word was sent to Camp Barrett, an army encampment only about 250 yards from the fuse works, where volunteer troops awaited deployment to Manila. A Lieutenant Yost of the Eighth California U.S. Infantry answered the call and dressed Sing's wounds. A police ambulance was summoned and word of the attack and the barricaded Chang was relayed to Alameda County Sheriff Calvin White. By the time White arrived, the ambulance had removed Ham Si Sing to the receiving hospital in Oakland, where a team of doctors set to work on him without much hope of success.

The records are unclear on exactly how many deputies initially came to the fuse works with Sheriff White, as various officers came and went throughout the day. Among those present early on were Will Moffitt, H.S. Smith, Harry Cramer, Jeremiah Quinlan and a deputy listed only as "Manning."

Seven other sheriff's men who went out to the Western Fuse and Explosives Company works early on July 18 would figure prominently in the incidents unfolding there. Six would be there when matters came to a head. Only one of those would survive. These seven were: Albert, Charles and Edgar White (sons of Sheriff White), Daniel Cameron, Joseph Lerri, George Woodsum, and Oakland Constable Gustave Koch.

Calvin Bailey White had been sheriff of Alameda County since winning election over legendary California lawman Harry Morse in 1894. White's eldest son, 29-year-old Albert Wesley White, had been a deputy since his father's election. The youngest, 21-year-old Edgar Howard White, was new to the job. Charles Milton White, middle of the three brothers, was 27. He was a motorman until his father took office in 1894, then he was hired as a deputy sheriff and appointed chief jailer. In June of 1897, Charles was in the news after a brewery workers' picnic at a local park became a drunken melee. Called on to restore order, Charles "alone kept at bay an angry, excited crowd and coolly faced a dozen leveled pistols." The *Oakland Tribune* wrote of Charles, "his unswerving loyalty and his keen sense of duty impressed all who met him, and it was to [sic] these qualities which have become so closely identified with him."

Daniel Carlyle Cameron was born April 10, 1860, in Centerville (part of modern day Fremont), twenty-four miles south of Oakland. He'd lived in the Bay Area his entire life. In early 1897 Sheriff White had appointed Cameron as a deputy "to serve especially in the court rooms," where his duties primarily involved serving papers. Upon his appointment, Cameron moved from the family ranch in Centerville to Oakland, where he roomed with an uncle. "The sheriff reposed much confidence in the young man," the *Oakland Tribune* said of him, "and frequently sent him on expeditions that required coolness, tact and unquestioned bravery."

Gustave Adolph Koch was born November 19, 1864, in Tuolumne, but had lived in Temescal – an Oakland suburb – since about 1873. A teamster by trade, he was elected constable of Oakland Township in 1894. Koch was a member of the Temescal Volunteer Fire Department, the Knights of Pythias, and San Francisco's Marine Yacht Club. He had been attached, in his official capacity, to Oakland Judge Frederick C. Clift's court. "He was brave and cool-headed," wrote the *Oakland Tribune*, "and thought nothing of danger when in the discharge of his duties. Many of the criminal class knew Koch and knew him but to fear him."

Like the Whites, George Clinton Woodsum was a native of Maine. Like Koch he was an avid sailor. Born November 8, 1864, Woodsum lived in Berkeley where he had served both as deputy town clerk and town clerk. Sheriff White appointed Woodsum a deputy sheriff in 1897. He served both in courtrooms and at the jail alongside Charles White. In early June 1898, Woodsum arrested a man named J.T. Richards who was "flourishing a pistol" on the street near Woodsum's home. After a brief scuffle, Woodsum "forced the pistol away and took him to the county jail." Per the *Tribune*, Woodsum was a "cool, daring man with no nervous apprehension of personal danger and was well qualified to be a peace officer."

Joseph John Lerri was perhaps the most experienced officer of the group. He was a native New Yorker, born in Brooklyn on November 16, 1854. His family moved to California the following year and Joe grew up in San Francisco, where he worked as a carpet layer. In 1884 he and his wife established a successful carpet laying/steam cleaning business in Oakland. Lerri had been a deputy sheriff since early 1894 when he was appointed by Calvin White's predecessor, Sheriff W.H.H. Hussey, "for humane work chiefly." In that capacity he'd handled such duties as monitoring, at the request of the local humane society, a pigeon shoot hosted by the Haywood Gun Club. The society had no objection to participants shooting the birds so long as they were killed. All apparently went well; the *San Francisco Call* noted, "there were no arrests made."

In July of 1895 Lerri was involved in a curious incident. While policing Emeryville's Shell Mound Park one evening, he became involved in some sort of altercation, and the individual he was tussling with struck him over the head with a club or stick. Dazed, Lerri fired twice at his fleeing assailant and one of his bullets struck 17-year-old Everett Spencer, who had been "frolicking" in the park with a couple of friends. The boys ran, and Lerri gave brief foot chase, but was quickly outrun and returned about his business, apparently unaware he'd shot Spencer. Spencer's friends loaded him onto a streetcar and took him to the receiving hospital. All three denied any connection with the assault on Lerri, claiming a case of mistaken identity. Although early newspaper reports said that Spencer had been "fatally wounded," he not only survived, but made a remarkably quick recovery. Lerri's bullet had struck the spine, and doctors were forced to leave a chunk of it embedded, but predicted no complications.

Although news reports don't record Lerri's side of the story, the fact that Spencer left the hospital two weeks later with no ill effects, and apparently no ill will, suggests that he and his pals may not have been the innocents they professed to be. In any case, Lerri was still on the job the following November when he and Charles White aided a posse of Contra Costa County deputies in the hunt for a convict escaped from Folsom prison. The *Oakland Tribune* characterized Lerri thus: "He was a brave man and was considered one of the best officers in the county."

Though Sheriff White and most of the deputies with him were reasonably seasoned lawmen, they could not have been prepared for the situation that faced them at the fuse works that day. Chang had built a barrier across the powder magazine doorway by stacking two twenty-five pound cans of powder atop a double row of fifty pound cans. Across the top of his barrier he'd laid a plank, possibly to prop the door open for ventilation – it was mid-July, after all. According to conflicting – and hotly disputed – reports, the magazine contained at that time anywhere from 4,000 to 40,000 pounds of gunpowder. The *San Francisco Call* summed things up succinctly: "The Chinaman has his revolver, hatchet and matches, and with 5,000 pounds of black powder makes an enemy that would awe any body of men."

Sheriff White and his deputies conferred with the fuse works officials at the scene; President Edward G. Lukens, Secretary Francis H. Pitman, and Superintendent Henry G. Prindle. The men told Sheriff White that they had made a couple of perfunctory attempts to talk Chang out, but he'd refused and was threatening to blow up the magazine. The officials were more or less cooperative, though the lawmen had great difficulty getting straight answers as to just what was stored in the magazine. All three claimed that there was no dynamite or other high explosives, while all dissembled as to how much powder was on hand. Prindle was the least cooperative. As direct supervisor, he was most likely to know how much powder was in the magazine, but he hemmed and hawed and frequently changed answers. It may be that he had something of a grudge against the Alameda County authorities; Prindle had been tried – and acquitted – for murder thirteen years earlier after shooting to death a doctor who had allegedly "taken improper liberties" with Mrs. Prindle. He'd been acquitted on an insanity plea then had returned (to no one's apparent concern) to his work supervising an explosives plant. Whether they knew Prindle's history on this date (and there's no indication they did) the officers were not impressed with the superintendent. In the gravity of the situation they all faced, Prindle found time to take offense and complain because Sheriff White had spoken to him without first dismounting his horse.

Issues with company officials aside, White and his men knew they were dealing with a potential disaster. Whatever the amount of powder – two tons or twenty – an explosion would be catastrophic. The officers hastily deliberated their course of action. Chang had made it plain that if anyone tried to remove him from his safe haven he would explode the magazine. He clearly had the means. The lawmen felt that Chang's preferred course, if he were given the opportunity, would be to slip out the magazine's rear window, scale the fence, and disappear. They decided that they should attempt to parley with Chang and negotiate surrender, but failing that, they would retreat into hiding, make Chang think he had a clear field, and take him when he tried to escape. Sheriff White gave his men two clear directives: Do not try to force Chang out, and do not under any circumstances allow him to escape. "When he stuck his head out to reconnoiter," the sheriff later recalled, "the men were to fire upon him, taking care especially not to shoot the powder." He was quick to add, "I felt that we would be perfectly justified in shooting down such a dangerous madman."

After stationing deputies with Winchester rifles, out of Chang's view, to watch the magazine, Sheriff White gave orders to evacuate civilians in and around the fuse works. He later confessed that this was done as much to lure Chang into believing the site was abandoned as it was for the safety of those individuals. Still, it would prove a wise precaution. The Chinese workers had mostly left by then; the remainder were advised to follow suit. Lukens and Pitman left also, while Prindle remained. Sheriff White and his deputies went door to door, asking occupants in neighboring homes and businesses to clear out. Most, once they learned the situation, were only too happy to oblige. They gathered belongings and sought temporary lodging in the city, or stayed with friends and family living at a safe distance. Some few merely set up camp in a vacant field several hundred yards away, or in empty boxcars along the railroad tracks some distance off.

About thirty-five families in all were moved out. As always, there were a few holdouts. One of these was Mrs. Sadie Hill, a 60-ish woman who lived at the King's Daughters' Home for Incurables in San Francisco, a well known sanatorium. She was staying with a Mrs. Pride, a neighbor of the Stephensons, and for unknown reasons she was "obdurate" with the officers and refused to leave.

After assisting his men in evacuating the fuse works and the surrounding neighborhood, Sheriff White returned to Oakland sometime in the late afternoon, leaving Albert White in charge. Edgar White, Koch, Lerri and Cramer left at some point also. The sheriff's plan to make the area appear deserted was frustrated throughout the afternoon by the arrival of various other individuals and groups, official and unofficial. Al White himself was guarding the gate to the plant when Secretary Pitman returned at about 5:30 p.m., intent on speaking with Chang and trying to coax him out of his stronghold. Pitman apparently arrived in the company of Ah Puck (called in other accounts We Puck or Quong Yong), the Chinese foreman of the plant, who had come from San Francisco to help. Puck had known Chang for twenty years, Pitman explained, and could speak to him in his native language.

Just as Pitman arrived, a Captain Baldwin marched over from Camp Barrett with a company of soldiers, offering assistance to the lawmen. When White explained to Baldwin the very negative effect the appearance of armed, uniformed troops might have upon Chang, the Captain took his point and marched the men back whence they came. Pitman was so confident that he could, via Puck, talk Chang into surrender that White agreed to let him try. By now, Chang was certainly under no illusion that he was alone on the grounds.

Pitman and Puck slowly approached the magazine. When they were ten yards from the door, Chang appeared behind his breastworks and halted them at gunpoint. Speaking through Puck, Pitman appealed to the barricaded man, promising he'd be treated fairly if he surrendered, and that the company would do all it could to assist him. Though Pitman "made him all kinds of inducements," Chang replied he would rather blow himself up than surrender. He swore that if escape proved impossible he would kill himself in two or three days. He urged Pitman to persuade the lawmen that they should leave the area and let him escape. Pitman promised to try, saying he could secure Chang "a chance to escape off our property at least." Chang allowed Puck to approach the doorway and pass him a $10 gold piece so he would have some traveling money, but remained unconvinced. Sometime between 6 p.m. and 7 p.m., Al White allowed Prindle, who had known Chang since he began working at the fuse works, to try his luck. He fared no better than Pitman. "The only answer Prindle received," wrote the *Oakland Tribune* the next day, "was an order to retire under pain of being shot to death himself."

As Prindle and Puck backed away, Chang called out to them that he was thirsty and would like some water. Prindle relayed the request to Al White. Deputy William Moffitt suggested to White that they dope the water with morphine then, once the drug took effect, simply go in and carry Chang out. Al thought the plan too risky; he was confident that they could wait Chang out. In any case, Puck, the only one Chang would permit to approach the magazine, refused to carry the water if it was tampered with in any way. Prindle took a glass to an outdoor faucet within Chang's line of sight and, to reassure him there was no monkey business, filled and emptied it several times. When Puck delivered the glass to Chang, the gunman was still suspicious; he merely rinsed out his mouth and spit the water on the ground.

Pitman made a final plea to Al White, stressing that Chang only wanted "a show to get over the fence." He suggested that White remove all deputies but one or, better still, let Chang escape and capture him later in Chinatown. Ah Puck, he said, had assured him that Chang would find no safe harbor in the Chinese community, but would be "turned over to the authorities five minutes after he arrived in San Francisco." Al White would consent to neither outlandish plan. He wasn't about to let an attempted murderer simply walk away. His father's orders had been clear.

There was no further interaction with Chang on July 18. As darkness approached, Prindle and Pitman left the site in time to catch the last electric train car for Oakland and home. Al White now returned to the original plan of making the fuse works appear deserted. He moved all his men outside the fence line in hopes that Chang would emerge from his hole. As the *San Francisco Call* reported, with the racial attitude typical of the times, the deputies "settled in to a long siege trusting to hunger and thirst to drive the desperate Mongol from his unique fortress." White and Smith were the last ones out the gate and made a great show of leaving, for Chang's benefit.

As time passed Al White became less comfortable with this arrangement. As soon as it was fully dark, he and Deputy Smith crept back over the fence and took up a position under a large willow tree twenty or thirty yards from the magazine. Lying prone, they were out of Chang's sight but were able to keep close watch on the doorway. Outside the fence, other deputies kept watch on the window. Monotonous hours crawled by with no activity until around 11 p.m. when Al heard a commotion from the road. He stealthily backtracked to the fence and saw a crowd of young men – boys, really – who'd come out to the site on a lark, hoping for a peek at a dangerous criminal. Al impressed upon them the danger to his men and to themselves and convinced them to move along. As the group left, he saw Gus Koch coming up the road, returning to assist. He showed Koch where to hop the fence and guided him to the vantage point under the tree, where they joined Smith and resumed their watch.

As Al White and his comrades kept their vigil, a team of doctors at Oakland's receiving hospital worked to save Ham Si Sing's life. Chang's pistol shot and the spectacles fragment had perforated his intestines in about ten places. After removing nearly two feet of damaged intestine, Dr. William S. Porter joined the remaining sections with a "Murphy button," a recent innovation that allowed a surgeon to quickly and efficiently perform such splices. The doctors also reattached Sing's ear and sutured his other wounds. Although he "stood the operation well," the doctors told news reporters that they held out little hope for his survival. Earlier in the afternoon Sing had been able to dictate a statement to Assistant District Attorney Alfonso Moore, Jr. In it Sing acknowledged that he knew he was dying and verified the basic facts of the case, naming Gung Ung Chang as his assailant. At around 12:30 a.m. on July 19, the doctors were proven correct. With a brother and nephew at his bedside, Ham Si Sing died.

Around 1:30 a.m. Al White heard a buggy coming down the road. Once again he crept his way to the fence. This time he found a party of deputies, ready to relieve him. In the buggy were Al's younger brothers Edgar and Charles, along with George Woodsum and Joe

Lerri. Also with them was Charley White's friend, Frederick Albert
Sherrott, a 25-year-old warehouse worker and newspaper vendor from
Oakland, who'd tagged along at Charley's invitation. Although not a
deputy, Sherrott was likely at some point that morning deputized,
either formally or informally. Presumably, the relief deputies brought
with them the news that Sing was dead.

Al White may have had some hesitation in turning the situation
over to his brothers. After briefing the group and passing on the
sheriff's orders to stay hidden and wait Chang out, he took his brother
Charley and George Woodsum aside. "You are both married men," he
said, "and if you have any hesitation, boys, don't go in." Charley
White responded, with younger brotherly bravado, "If you can go in, I
guess we can."

As Al White and Smith prepared to leave, Koch told Al, "The last
car has gone, and I might as well stay." This was welcome news;
though Koch, at 33, wasn't the oldest officer in the group (Lerri was
43; Cameron was 38), White knew the constable was "cool and level-
headed, and would keep them quiet." Leaving his brother Charles and
Joe Lerri to maintain the position inside the yard with Koch, Al had
his brother Ed, Woodsum, Cameron, Moffitt and Sherrott take
positions outside the fence, as far as 150 yards from the magazine.
He advised Koch that when dawn approached they should retreat
toward the gate, keeping the building between them and Chang. He
gave Smith's Winchester to his brother Charles. Placing Charley
technically in charge of the group, Al White left the fuse works, along
with Deputies Smith and Manning.

Little is more trying on an officer's nerves – and patience – than a
stakeout where nothing at all happens. This was the situation for
Charley White and the others throughout the early hours of July 19.
The combination of adrenalin and boredom was no doubt wearing the
officers down when Constable Stephenson, who'd remained in his
home after his family had left, came over around 4:30 a.m. with a
welcome offer. He approached Ed White and Sherrott as they lay in a

trench along the road watching the magazine's window and invited all the men into his house for coffee and breakfast. The cold, tired deputies were grateful and went in shifts to partake. While they were there, some of the deputies – it's not clear which – reportedly discussed the idea of rushing the magazine, knocking down Chang's barricade, and dragging him out before he could do any harm.

For nearly an hour the men took turns going to Stephenson's for a bite to eat and a bracing cup of coffee. As they returned, Charles White, Lerri, Woodsum and Cameron entered the fuse works yard. Charley White had evidently decided to abandon any pretense that Chang was alone. Ed White and Sherrott returned to their trench just outside the fence line. According to later testimony, Chang saw Charles White and hailed him to approach the magazine. With Lerri at his side, White went within twenty feet of the magazine to talk with Chang. He asked if Chang was hungry. He was. Charley asked when he intended to come out, and Chang responded that he would come out "in a couple of days."

From their vantage point on the window, Fred Sherrott and Ed White couldn't see the magazine door but could hear snatches of conversation between Chang and Charley White. Since Chang obviously wasn't coming out the window, Sherrott whispered to Ed, "Come along and let's see what they are doing." The two left their trench and tiptoed to a spot nearer the magazine, where they could peer through knotholes in the fence. Sherrott could see Charley White and Joe Lerri standing together five or six yards from the magazine, talking with Chang through the open door. Woodsum stood immediately behind them and Cameron was about a hundred feet away, near the willow tree. "I thought he was perfectly safe at that distance," Sherrott would later say, "as I had been told that the black powder would not hurt anybody 100 feet off." Sherrott could not see Koch but "knew he was somewhere in the yard, ready to shoot."

Both Sherrott and Ed White could now see and hear the negotiation taking place at the magazine. Charley White was telling Chang that Sing was still alive and that it would be best for everyone if he would come out. Though he promised Chang wouldn't be hurt, Sherrott and Ed both knew, Sherrott said later, that if and when Chang came out he'd be fired upon "if he showed the least inclination to get away or resist." Now they realized that if that happened, they were in the line of Charley White's and Lerri's fire. Not only that but, according to Sherrott, "I wanted to get into a position where I could get a shot at him myself, and where he could not shoot me with his pistol." He said, "Come on, Eddy," and he and the younger White brother ran for the High Street gate.

As the two men were on the move, it appeared Charles White had convinced Chang to stand down. Chang was stepping outside the door as Fred Sherrott and Ed White entered the yard. Charley White and Joe Lerri were inching closer. Whether something spooked Chang, he had a change of heart, or he simply decided his gambler's luck had run out, he began to backtrack. Witnesses later reported him shouting, "Go away, I blow you up!" Some claimed that Lerri sprang towards the door and tried to shut it before Chang could reenter; Ed White denied that anyone touched the door, saying "that would have been foolhardiness." Whatever happened, Chang ducked back inside the magazine and slammed the door behind him. Exactly what he did inside will never be known, but the result was something all parties who lived to tell about it agreed upon.

One account of the incident put it very briefly: "It was exactly 5:18 o'clock on the morning of July 19, 1898, when the hand of one man dealt a death-blow the like of which perhaps history has never known." It may have been an understatement at that. Whether he had touched it off by pistol, match or fuse, within seconds of reentering the magazine, Gung Ung Chang unleashed a hellish explosion. Fred Sherrott and Edgar White, both some eighty feet away when the blast occurred, were hurled over twenty yards. White was knocked unconscious for some time, both his and Sherrott's faces were "somewhat disfigured by flying debris," and Sherrott was badly injured in the groin. He picked himself up only to witness a scene from Dante's Inferno. The entire fuse works – nine buildings in all – was gone, reduced to scattered piles of flaming debris, and there was no sign of the officers who'd been standing near it.

The concussion was felt in Oakland, of course, where downtown buildings rocked and swayed and folks assumed there'd been an earthquake. It was felt five miles off on the far side of Alameda to the south, and Berkeley to the north. They felt it in Sausalito, thirty miles across the water, and down in San Jose, beyond the southern end of San Francisco Bay, over forty miles away. Closer to home, row upon row of tents at Camp Barrett were mown down like wheat before a scythe, and dozens of troops who were knocked off their feet were convinced the Spanish fleet had sailed into the bay and laid siege. A sentry at the camp later described a dense cloud of dust and smoke rising hundreds of feet into the air and "many thousand pieces of timber and rock" falling. "The adjacent country," wrote the *Oakland Tribune* was "deluged with a rain of sparks and dismantled timber, and many narrow escapes from injury took place."

Along with Ed White and Fred Sherrott, several civilians whose homes adjoined the fuse works were injured, though none seriously. Of the sheriff's officers, only Will Moffitt, who had remained outside the fence line, escaped unscathed.

Troops at Camp Barrett had seen one body "hurled high in the air and…deposited in the great mass of debris" a hundred feet away. They hurried to the spot and reached, just ahead of the flames, "the still-breathing body of Cameron." Of the deputies closest to the magazine, only Dan Cameron had escaped death. It was not a fortunate escape; his body was so horribly mangled he could at first only be identified by the overcoat he wore. His face was badly cut and bruised and while one side of his body was intact, the other was "one lacerated and contused mass." Worst, he'd been impaled on the branches of a tree – apparently the same willow tree the officers had lain under earlier. Though he would be rushed to the receiving hospital in Oakland, Cameron would die soon after arrival.

Sheriff White, riding horseback, had been returning to the works from Oakland when the blast nearly threw him from his startled mount. He was in no doubt about what had happened. Though keenly aware that two of his sons were at the site, the sheriff's first thought was to summon assistance. He galloped for the nearest telephone to call for the fire department and police ambulances. Only after attending to this duty did Sheriff White continue on to the fuse works, to learn there that one son had survived and one had not.

U.S. Army troops from nearby Camp Barrett aided in searching through the rubble for survivors and victims. *(Author's Collection)*

As quickly as they could muster, two companies of troops under command of a Captain Carrington double-timed over from Camp Barrett to fight fires and aid the search for victims and survivors.

Firefighting was a daunting task. What little remained of the buildings was fully engulfed, and there was no fire fighting apparatus or any adequate water source. "As a consequence," the *Tribune* reported, "the flames ran riot and licked up everything they touched." The troops did manage to avert a second disaster, probably saving untold lives.

Six linked box cars standing on the Southern Pacific tracks just north of the works had escaped complete destruction by the blast, though most were badly damaged. In the midst of the group was one intact car, still loaded with several hundred fifty-pound cans of powder. Three of the damaged cars were burning and the flames were spreading toward the powder car. A group of soldiers rushed to the tracks and swiftly uncoupled the burning cars from the others which, "with the strong shoulders of many of the boys in blue behind them, were sent rolling at a lively gait down the track out of danger."

When Oakland and Alameda Fire Department crews arrived they had some difficulty in wresting control from the enthusiastic soldiers, and only "after a vigorous assertion of their authority" did they take charge of the firefighting, relegating to the troops the grimmer tasks of recovery. The firemen were awed at the devastation they saw. Any sign of the magazine where Gung Ung Chang had made his deadly stand was gone. In its place was a crater twenty feet deep.

West of the magazine had been the reeling house, filled with reels of the finished product and barrels of tar used to coat fuse. North of this had been the mixing plant, and further north the engine room, of which only a brick enclosure surrounding the boiler still stood. West of this had been a long wooden shed filled with boxes and paper used in shipping; adjoining it was a corrugated metal building where tightly packed rolls of cotton cloth used in fuse making had been kept.

These last two were a particular problem for the firemen; the sheet metal had been stripped from the latter by the blast and the volatile cotton cloth and paper goods had been "reduced to a molten mass of lava-like material with a glow in intensity of the fuel of Tartarus." Added to all of this, mountains of heaped coal, kept for stoking the engine room boiler, were burning like Hell's own furnace. The fire departments' combined equipment was simply insufficient.

At first word of the explosion, Edward Lukens had left his San Francisco home for the site. He helped organize and manage the tasks underway, directing the search for victims and survivors, and established a guard around the perimeter to control the droves of curiosity seekers who'd begun converging almost immediately.

The crater at the right of this photo was all that remained of the powder magazine where Gung Ung Chang had barricaded himself. *(Author's Collection)*

As word spread, so many onlookers came out, anxious for a glimpse of the destruction, that the electric railway lines crisscrossing the area were overflowing, and the roads around Melrose so choked with vehicles that they were all but impassable. "The spectacle was uninspiring," the *Oakland Tribune* remarked on these sight-seeing excursions.

The paper wasn't referring to detonation craters, shattered buildings, or burning railroad cars, but to the human toll. For as soon as those at the scene began looking for – and occasionally finding – survivors, they began also to find the remains of those less fortunate. One of the first such finds was made by Fred Sherrott, who came upon one of Charles White's arms lying about 200 feet from where he'd stood talking to Chang. Ed White had searched in vain for signs of his brother, finding only tattered remnants of his coat. "Little by little," Sherrott said, "we found other fragments but undoubtedly much of the remains were consumed by the fire."

Cameron, of course, was accounted for. The remains of Lerri, Woodsum, Koch and Charley White would be found scattered over a 300-yard radius around the crater left by Chang. Most of Charley White's remains – what the *Oakland Tribune* bluntly called "the back of the body" – were found furthest from the spot. He was 300 yards south of the magazine, identified by his shredded clothing and by his billy club, which was found nearby. A portion of his left side was found in the ruins of a house across the road. Woodsum had been catapulted some 200 yards north and landed on the railroad tracks. He could be recognized only by a ring on the finger of one mangled hand, a belt he wore, and "the scalp and one ear which cling to the remains."

Lerri's body was found horrifically mutilated under rubble near the Stephenson house. His body was missing hands and feet. Only clothing fragments and an immovable finger joint – an old injury – on what remained of his right hand served to identify him. Gus Koch's body was found remarkably intact, his rifle still at his side, in the smoldering rubble a mere 75 feet from the blast site. He appeared to have been killed by the sheer concussion and, except for "a swollen face, which bears a pained expression," his body had none of the ghastly signs of trauma that those of his fellow officers bore.

Despite the officers' precautions the earlier evening, there was one citizen among the fatalities. Crews digging through the piles of wood and plaster that had been homes found the body of Mrs. Sadie Hill, the "obdurate" visitor from San Francisco, buried under the shambles of the Stephenson house. She had apparently, and mercifully, been sleeping, and was killed by a "death-dealing blow" from debris striking the right side of her head. Though her body had been somewhat torn and disjointed by falling timbers, its owner had felt no pain.

Many private homes and businesses around the perimeter of the fuse works sustained damage or were destroyed in the blast. *(Author's Collection)*

Considering the number of people killed within the deadly 600-yard circle, it was little short of a miracle that most survived, and that injuries were relatively few and minor. That White and Sherrott survived, albeit with injuries and nerves "unstrung by the horror of the scene," almost surpasses belief. There were several minor injuries to nearby residents, all of whom who fared better than their homes. Mrs. E. E. McLean, a "well-known hair doctor," awoke from the blast and was slashed on the neck by flying glass. Her brother narrowly escaped decapitation by a broken sheet of plate glass that skimmed edgewise through the air just above his head and shattered against his bedpost. Perry Wilson, a carpenter who lived across from the works, was slammed into the floor of his home when the magazine exploded.

Saloonkeeper George Giblin, who lost both his business and his home to the blast, was hurt by flying debris. His wife was home at the time and escaped with minor injuries after she, like the unfortunate Sadie Hill, was buried beneath the falling remains of the Stephenson house. Another neighbor, Charles Romer, had been going out to milk a cow when the concussion hurled both him and the cow twenty feet away and reduced his barn to splinters. Remembering that there were ladies present in some of the adjacent houses, Romer crawled through the debris and brought Mrs. Giblin out to safety.

As for Gung Ung Chang, there was little of the murderer to be found. Though both the Oakland and San Francisco papers delighted in reporting that only Chang's "queue," or pigtail, was found – one report even claiming that the young boy who found it sold it to a souvenir hunter for a dollar – there seems little substance to such fanciful accounts. No such item was listed among the various body fragments later attributed to Chang in the morgue at Oakland.

Throughout the day as crews and volunteers picked through the rubble they found various other bits of evidence – mortal and otherwise – that gave mute testimony to the devastation that had taken place. Deputy Will Moffitt, who alone among the lawmen had escaped uninjured, was of great assistance in locating and identifying the remains of his fallen comrades. Miscellaneous body parts collected and sent to the morgue for later identification included a right hand found a hundred feet from Woodsum's body, a rib found on the railroad tracks nearly a half mile away, and a section of upper jaw with five teeth remaining. The latter, owing to some distinctive dental repairs, was believed to be George Woodsum's. In contrast to the pigtail story, a mangled right foot found 300 yards from the crater, several scattered vertebrae, and a section of spinal column lying near a canal half a mile distant, were thought to be from Chang.

There were less grisly finds as well: Charles White's rifle, "twisted but recognizable;" a hinge from the magazine door found on Fruitvale Avenue, half a mile from the site; and a bloody dirk that, according to Chang's cousin, belonged to the killer himself. This led to speculation that Chang had stabbed himself before touching off the blast, though a man about to blow himself to mist committing suicide by knife seems a bit improbable.

As generally happens in incidents like this, the questions almost immediately shifted from "What happened?" to "Who is to blame?" The day of the disastrous explosion Lukens gave the *San Francisco Call* a statement mourning "The untimely deaths of those brave men," and concluded by saying "this is no time to express any opinion as to the wisdom of their course." Yet within days he'd be blaming the officers outright, and considering a lawsuit against Alameda County to recover damages. The *Call* itself couldn't resist a bit of editorializing: "There can be no question," it said, "that the officers were over-confident and imprudent. Had they not kept so close a guard, had they gone out of sight and allowed the murderer to have escaped from the building and from the grounds there would have been no mourning hearts in Alameda today." The paper criticized Al White's decision (although attributing it to Charles) not to drug the water given to Chang. Never mind that it wouldn't have worked, and might have provoked him into blowing up the magazine sooner, while company employees were still on site. "His misplaced idea of humanity," the *Call* suggested, "cost him and his brave companions their lives."

While fingers were pointing at Sheriff White's men, the surviving officers who were at the fuse works on July 18 nursed suspicions that they'd been misled about what sort of powder, and how much, had been in the magazine. Some claimed dynamite had been stored there. Some said they remembered Secretary Pitman saying the powder was not explosive (Pitman naturally denied this). The *Oakland Tribune* at least considered the possibility, and suggested that if the officers "had been given to understand that the powder was only burning powder, it would tend to explain why they went towards [sic] the magazine with such confidence."

Whether or not the county officers' suspicions were warranted, company officials immediately closed ranks. Lukens said publicly that he'd feared this result all along, and made clear that he had "warned the deputy sheriffs against a rash movement." Pitman called the officers "overzealous" and said that if they had followed his advice there would have been no catastrophe. Prindle continued to give evasive answers about the quantity of gunpowder. When Al White and Jeremiah Quinlan visited the fuse works on the 20th, they had a "warm conversation" with the superintendent. Both men recalled Prindle telling the officers two days earlier that there were twenty tons of powder stockpiled in the magazine. Now, with "violent language and much gesticulation," Prindle was denying it. When White pressed the point, Prindle insisted he'd never mentioned a specific amount. "I don't propose to get into trouble by being misquoted," he snarled, though his behavior suggests he was more afraid of being *accurately* quoted. He became so irate that at one point he challenged Quinlan to fight, an invitation the deputy calmly – if reluctantly – declined. Prindle would not even answer queries as to how much powder the defunct magazine was *capable* of storing; he replied "with undiminished vehemence" that he didn't know.

For his part Sheriff White was inclined to assign responsibility to both sides and most of all, of course, to Chang. He was astute enough not to accuse W.F.E.C. outright of storing dynamite or giant powder – any proof, after all, had been obliterated – but he did say he believed "an unusual amount had been kept on hand." He said Pitman had assured him there was not sufficient powder in the magazine "to cost great or general damage, even should it be fired."

The sheriff acknowledged that his son Charles "was too impetuous," and speculated that he had likely become "tired of lying on the cold ground awaiting developments and tried to get the fellow out. He permitted himself to be drawn into a trap." If he had to do it again, White said, he would put a cordon of guards around a half-mile perimeter and starve his man out. White may have spoken as a father bragging about his sons, a sheriff boasting of his men, or both, when he said, "my boys never shirked duty on account of danger." He touched on what critics of the officers' actions failed to appreciate, or at least to acknowledge: If the deputies *had* rushed the magazine when Chang came out, they probably believed it was their last, best chance to avert a tragedy. They ran toward danger when most would have run away.

At the morgue in Oakland the victims' remains, such as they were, were sorted, identified as best they could be, and examined by Dr. Porter in preparation for the coroner's inquest to be held at 7 p.m. on the 20th. Widows, relatives and friends coming to identify the dead had to run a gauntlet of morbidly curious onlookers who had congregated around the building and were only kept at bay by a "strict blockade." Viewing the remains was a grim, unenviable task and could only have magnified the anguish loved ones were already feeling. Cameron's, Koch's and Sadie Hill's remains were unsightly enough; of the others the *Tribune* did not exaggerate in saying, "There is no resemblance in the remains to any human being. They rather appear chaotic masses of jellied flesh, bones and rags." Still, the identification was necessary. Though a legal necessity, the inquest was in this case mostly a formality; there was little question what had occurred, and Chang wouldn't be standing trial. Yet there were other considerations. Several of the men carried life insurance and the companies would not pay without positive proof of decease. One of these was George Woodsum, whose dentist Dr. J.A. Hutton was called upon to identify the jaw fragment by dental work he had performed.

The victims' bodies were laid out on slabs and treated with as much delicacy and respect as the proceedings allowed. Not so their killer. "In marked contrast to the care of these bodies," observed the *Tribune*, "lie unnoticed the bloody fragments that once composed the body of Gong [sic] Ung Chang. They are thrown into a box and are despised contents. Piece by piece during the day, this pile has increased as here and there small bits have been found." There were puzzles; Dr. Porter reported that a right ear he believed to be from a white male did not belong to any of the victims. This raised the possibility, apparently never resolved, of an unknown eighth fatality.

Once the examinations and identifications were complete, the remains were released for burial. What was done with Chang's remains is not recorded; presumably they were turned over to family. Cameron and Koch would be buried privately by their families; Cameron's body was sent to his father in Centerville and Koch's to his family's home in Alameda. Mrs. Hill's body was returned to the King's Daughters' Home in San Francisco. The remaining deputies would be interred after a public memorial service being planned by a committee of Alameda County officials.

The inquest on the evening of the 20th brought few surprises. The coroner, Dr. Robert O. Baldwin, and a jury of ten men heard testimony from the surviving White brothers, Fred Sherrott, Charles Stephenson and Perry Wilson, as well as from W.F.E.C. officials

Lukens, Prindle and Pitman. Al White, the first witness, recounted the events of the 18th and said he had directed his brother Charles and the other deputies not to try and force Chang out but cautioned them "don't lose him in any event." Al corroborated his father's statements that Pitman had downplayed the hazards. Pitman, Al White claimed, said that the powder "might blow the roof off the magazine and injure some of the buildings nearby but it would not kill the officers."

The *San Francisco Call* felt that from the jurors' questions "it was very evident" that they believed too much powder had been kept in storage and that the company had been negligent in allowing Chang ready access to it. Pitman told the jury he did not know how much powder was in the magazine on July 18 – not more than two-and-a-half tons, he thought – and that it was all black powder. He claimed that there were never more than 200 kegs on hand, and said that at the time of the explosion "a consignment was on the track but not unloaded." Pitman said the company used about 500 pounds of powder per day.

Prindle, who was more likely to know, claimed that they used only around 200 pounds per day. He said that he'd last done inventory on July 1, and he estimated that at that time there were over six tons on hand. Prindle said that he told the officers on July 18 that there was no dynamite, only "black military powder." He insisted that he hadn't told the officers how much powder was stored, but now said "there might have been 200 twenty-five pound cans." The jurors found Prindle's answers unsatisfactory, but were never able to pin him down. When Lukens' turn came he claimed to have no knowledge of how much powder was kept in stock, saying that "such matters were left to the Superintendent." If their testimony is to be believed, it seems the only W.F.E.C. employee who knew for certain what was in the magazine on July18 was Gung Ung Chang.

Fred Sherrott testified that as he and Edgar White approached the gate, Lerri lunged towards the magazine door and tried to shut it but that because of the powder cans Chang had stacked, "it seemed to jam and he could not close it." This allowed Chang to retreat inside, he said, "and then the explosion came." Perry Wilson, the injured carpenter, claimed that he had seen the officers trying to force the door open with a plank just before the blast.

The jury spent significant time questioning the company's employees about access to the magazine and its deadly contents. Officials and workers alike testified that the magazine was kept unlocked during the workday, so that powder could be removed as needed. Prindle testified that due to Chang's work in the spinning room he had unrestricted access to the magazine, implying that other workers did not. An employee named Fong Hing stated, however, that in his eight years at the works he had often been inside the magazine, although his duties did not require it.

"With a discussion on the methods of the company in allowing the Chinaman to have free access to the magazine," reported the *San Francisco Call*, "the evidence closed." The jury deliberated for half an hour without settling on a verdict. The sticking point seemed to be what culpability, if any, the company bore in the deaths. The jury determined to visit the site of the tragedy the next morning, then to reconvene and try to reach a conclusion.

On July 21 the coroner's jury met at the fuse works site and surveyed the devastation. Afterward, they assembled and heard additional testimony. Al White recounted Prindle's belligerent attitude on July 18 when the sheriff dared speak to the superintendent from horseback. Al testified that Prindle told him at that time the magazine contained twenty tons of black powder, which was direct contradiction to the company line now that it was not over than two-and-a-half. Deputy Quinlan testified briefly, corroborating Al White's statements.

Prindle was recalled and pointedly questioned on safety issues. He testified that the magazine was outside the Oakland city limits (a requirement of state law) and when asked if he felt that public safety was "sufficiently considered" in keeping the magazine unlocked and accessible, he said that he did.

After deliberating for an additional hour, the jury at last returned its verdict. Though it had seemed inclined to assign the company at least partial responsibility, the jury ruled simply that the victims had died from an explosion caused "with murderous intent by one Chinese named Quong Chung [sic]." Their verdict took only a minor dig at the company in pointing out that Chang was "an employee of said powder company with free access to said powder magazine."

In a separate proceeding the same coroner's jury ruled that Ham Si Sing (called "Ham She Son" in the verdict) died from "hemorrhage and shock caused by gunshot and hatchet wounds inflicted by Quong Chank [sic]."

It is possible the jury's attention to W.F.E.C.'s procedures was motivated in part by the fact that the company had publicly announced its intention to sue Alameda County for losses which Lukens estimated at around $200,000 (about 5.5 million in current dollars). There had been no insurance – their industry was uninsurable. All nine of the fuse works buildings had been destroyed and only about $2,000 worth of fuse materials, Lukens claimed, were salvageable.

While legal issues were being considered, Alameda County was mourning its fallen officers. There had been a great public outpouring of concern and sympathy for the surviving loved ones; Charles White's widow even received a moving condolence message from prisoners confined in the Alameda County Jail. On the afternoon of July 20, before the inquest, a committee of county officials had met at the Oakland Courthouse to plan "fitting ceremonials" honoring the slain officers. Though Cameron and Koch would be buried elsewhere after private ceremonies the next day, the memorial service the committee planned for the 22nd would recognize all five officers. The County Board of Supervisors met in special session on the 21st to pass resolutions in honor of its officers. Flags were to be lowered to half mast throughout the county, and government business was to be suspended to the extent possible until after the funerals. Elsewhere in the county, the city of Berkeley would pay tribute to resident George Woodsum by closing public offices and private businesses at noon on the 22nd and by detailing a "large body of firemen and lodge members" to attend the service in Oakland. The Albert Volunteer Fire Company, in which Woodsum had served, draped its firehouse in black crepe and passed a resolution in tribute to its brother.

At 1:30 p.m. on July 22, the vast, solemn procession assembled in front of the county courthouse, ready to proceed to Oakland's First Congregational Church. This gathering was soon joined by the firemen, fraternal members, friends and relations who had met at noon in Berkeley and marched in formation the five miles to Oakland. "Not since the birth of the city forty-six years ago," wrote the *San Francisco Call*, "has there been such a general demonstration of respect as was shown to the remains of the brave fellows who died doing their duty."

The ceremonies were indeed impressive. The cortege was led by a column of Oakland police officers "in full but draped uniform," led by Chief Willard Fletcher and two captains, Frank Carson and Adelbert Wilson. Following them were three Alameda County Superior Court judges – "the first time," the *Call* pointed out, "that the bench of Alameda County has ever marched on foot at any public funeral." Behind the judges came the county supervisors, then the heads of each county government department and their deputies. The most prominent of the latter, of course, was the Sheriff's Department. Close behind the county officials followed "a body of Oakland's most prominent citizens numbering several hundred." After this solemn escort came three horse-drawn hearses driving abreast down the broad boulevard. The center hearse carried Charles White's body; those flanking it bore Lerri and Woodsum. To the rear of the hearses members of the Knights of Pythias, Woodmen of the World and sundry other fraternal orders marched in formation, "all with draped flags and insignia." At the far end of this lengthy and august assembly came a "vast string of vehicles reaching several blocks, in which were people from all over the county."

The massive procession moved up Broadway to Fourteenth, up Washington over to Twelfth, and up Clay, ending at the church. The streets along every foot of the route were lined with crowds of quiet, mournful citizens who'd come out to pay final tribute to their sworn protectors. The turnout was unprecedented, and largely unanticipated. The church was already packed with well-wishers when the procession arrived, so that by the time the service was underway, "every aisle and every corner was jammed with people, while thousands were forced to remain outside." But remain they did, even though the late July heat could not have made things pleasant, outside or in.

Inside the church was a mass of floral offerings dwarfed by a piece sent jointly by the county officials – a nine foot high banner of white, decked with purple dried flowers spelling out the inscription "Brave and True – C.M. White, George C. Woodsum, D.C. Cameron, J.J. Lerri, Gus Koch."

The church service began at 2:00 p.m. sharp, as church and firehouse bells citywide tolled non-stop until 3 p.m. It was a lengthy service; due to the multiple decedents several different clergymen were in attendance and would speak. Their remarks came after hymns by the church choir, prayers, and a Masonic quartet singing "Sleep Thy Last Sleep." The Reverend Dr. Pierce of Berkeley, representing Woodsum's lodge, gave a brief address. He was followed by the Rev. Dr. E.R. Dille, who concluded by remarking of the officers, "They have done their duty and died for it and no man can do more." Dr. E. S. Chapman delivered a moving eulogy. He began by discussing the "deep significance in all this solemn pageantry," then went on to praise the bravery and self-sacrifice of those who knowingly and willingly put themselves in harm's way to protect others. His concluding remarks ably described the lot of every peace officer at that time, before, and since: "We rest securely in our homes and rejoice in the value of our possessions, too often indifferent to the dangers which confront the men whom we have placed on guard and by whose unfaltering fidelity in the midst of every peril our interests are kept in security."

After the memorial, Charles White's remains were cremated and interred at San Francisco's Odd Fellows cemetery in its majestic three-story Columbarium. Charles had died a newlywed, having married Dollie Rowland in March of 1897. Cameron was unmarried; he left behind his aged father – a Centerville rancher – and four married sisters: two in Centerville and two in Sacramento. He was buried in the Irvington Cemetery under the auspices of the Eden Parlor of the Native Sons of the Golden West. Gus Koch was unmarried; he left behind an elderly father living in Columbia, California, and two brothers and two sisters living in San Francisco. Woodsum belonged to both the Odd Fellows and Woodmen of the World. He left behind a wife and two children – a nine year old son and a five year old daughter. Joe Lerri left the largest family - a wife and eight children – one grown daughter, and seven boys and girls at home. Misfortune seemed to follow the Lerri clan, as the years ahead would demonstrate.

While the public was praising and honoring the late officers' bravery and sacrifice, serious issues were being raised with regard to the Western Fuse and Explosives Company. "Much dissatisfaction is expressed," the *San Francisco Call* reported on July 20, "by those who have suffered from the explosion as they believe that the company had far more powder on the premises than the law allows." Within days of the explosion an ad hoc group called the "Melrose Protective Association" held a meeting, chaired by Charles Stephenson, to discuss lawsuits against W.F.E.C. for damaged and destroyed homes. The 150 members raised $1,500 toward hiring the prominent Oakland law firm of George Reed and Emil Nusbaumer – former Alameda County district attorney and assistant district attorney – to represent them. The group contended that the company was negligent in allowing "such a dangerous man" as Chang access to its powder magazine. Within a week, residents of Melrose and the neighboring subdivisions of Fruitvale and Lockwood came together to draft and circulate a petition against allowing W.F.E.C. to rebuild the fuse works on the original site. The members presented their petition at an August meeting of the Board of Supervisors. Though sympathetic, the board pleaded that it had no legal standing to prevent reconstruction.

It was a moot point. Western Fuse and Explosives Company would never rebuild its works; owing to losses from the explosion and the costs of defending a barrage of resultant lawsuits, the company passed out of corporate existence seven years later. The lawsuits, meanwhile, would drag on for nearly twenty years. The most hard fought of the cases, brought by Melrose residents Frederick and Lisetta Kleebauer, would end in the California Supreme Court. The court spoke the final word on fault in the case, declaring that the company's storage of powder did not constitute a "nuisance" and ruling that the "explosion was caused by no act of the company, and resulted in a cause entirely beyond its control."

Over thirty suits for damages were filed against W.F.E.C., with individual claims ranging from $150.00 to $3,000. Complaints ranged from negligence to storing unsafe quantities of powder, and some alleged that – despite continual company denials – dynamite and nitroglycerin had also been stored in the magazine. The company's team of lawyers used every manner of legal maneuver to delay and obstruct cases for a score of years. At one point Lukens' stock was transferred to his son, George Russell Lukens, who was a state senator and thus could not be sued for damages. Meanwhile Prindle, who'd professed so little knowledge at the inquest into the five officers' deaths, testified as "an expert on the manufacture of all kinds of fuse" in a 1907 case involving the attempted murder by dynamite of Alameda Superior Court Judge F.B. Ogden.

Ultimately, none of the injured parties received much, if any, redress from the courts. In the end they had to content themselves with the fact that the W.F.E.C. was no more. Little comfort it must have been to them, and none whatever to the families of the murdered lawmen.

Sheriff White, who had lost one (and nearly two) sons, continued in office through 1898. Carrying out his day-to-day duties must have brought constant painful reminders. The *San Francisco Call* reported a poignant example on July 26, a week after the tragedy. The sheriff had presented the Board of Supervisors with "a requisition for four pairs of handcuffs and four deputy sheriff badges to take the place of those destroyed with the deputies last week." It was a mundane administrative action that must surely have caused Calvin White great heartache. In other routine matters, at the same board meeting, Deputy Constable Edward Weidlar and a J.C. Williamson each applied for Gus Koch's vacant Oakland Township position. Elsewhere, Woodsum's wife petitioned the court for her husband's business and real estate holdings in Berkeley.

One family particularly hard hit by the tragedy was Joe Lerri's. The *Oakland Tribune* remarked that "the blood fell no heavier on any home than this," and it was certainly true. Five weeks after Joe's death, three-year-old George Lerri fell under an incoming Southern Pacific train. He miraculously escaped injury, his tiny body having fallen into a shallow trough left by the recent removal of some ties. It was a freak occurrence with no connection at all to his father's death. Still, it might have been a sign that all was not destined to go well for the Lerris. They were in suitable financial shape; Joe had left his wife $10,000 in life insurance and a thriving business. But while Honora Lerri continued to operate the carpet cleaning firm, combined with the difficulty of raising seven children alone it may have been more than she could manage. A year and a half later she attempted to have her teenage daughters, Cerenia and Honora, committed to the Whittier Reform School as incorrigibles, telling the court that the pair tended to "stay out late of nights and run about." Her hearing before Judge F.B. Ogden (of Prindle's dynamite case) made public a bitter family feud over the daughters' upbringing. Joe Lerri's mother, Mrs. John Miller, claimed the girls were "simply following their mother's example," and told the *Call*, "I believe that when my son went out to the powder works he did not intend to ever come back. He wanted to get rid of his life and his miserable surroundings." Money, it turned out, was behind the enmity between Lerri's mother and his wife. Mrs. Miller claimed to have loaned Joe a large sum before he died and was eager to have it back. In the end, with the apparent consent of all adults involved, the daughters went to foster homes. In June of 1904, sixteen-year-old Edward Lerri was arrested in Oakland for attempted robbery, after the botched street mugging of a Chinese merchant. Newspapers reported that young Edward wept openly at his arraignment. In October of the same year, Edward's twenty-year-old brother, Vincent, "in a fit of boyish despondency," tried to kill himself by taking strychnine. In March of 1911, mourning for a wife who had died two years before, Vincent succeeded in killing himself by turning up the gas jets in his room.

When Sheriff White and his men answered the call of duty at the Western Fuse and Explosives Company that fateful summer day, they went into a desperate and unprecedented situation that nothing they had seen or done in the past could have fully prepared them to encounter. They were men from various walks of life, various ages, and various levels of experience, but they had one thing in common; they were answering the call of duty. Perhaps the best eulogy for the officers who died there came from the public statement offered by the committee that had planned their impressive memorial. The words are as true today as they were then. The statement said, in part "honorably they lived, bravely they died; the heritage of a noble example left by them will bear fruit when our generation has gone to join them."

EXTRA Oakland Tribune. **5th Edition**

VOL. LXXXVI.   OAKLAND, CALIFORNIA, TUESDAY EVENING, JULY 19, 1898.   NO. 194

SIX BLOWN TO ETERNITY

THE DEATH ROLL.

CHARLES WHITE, eldest son of Sheriff White.
GUS KOCH, Constable of Oakland Township.
J. J. LERRI, Deputy Sheriff.
GEO. C. WOODSUM, Deputy Sheriff, Berkeley.
D. C. CAMERON, Deputy Sheriff.
MRS. HILL, of San Francisco.
The murderous Chinese was also killed.

Murderous Chinese Fires the Fuse Works' Magazine.

Held at Bay, He Causes the Explosion Which Kills Five Officers, One Woman and Blows Himself Into Atoms.

The *Oakland Tribune* ran a special evening edition on July 19, 1898, with several full pages devoted to the tragedy at Melrose. *(Author's Collection)*

These sketches from the *San Francisco Chronicle* show four of the five officers killed at the Western Fuse and Explosives Company plant. *(Author's Collection)*

Chapter 8: *"Papa, did you kill Grandma?"*
Sheriff John Henry Dillingham
Platte County, Missouri (August 20, 1900)

To most people, America's war on drugs might seem to be a purely modern concern, and a mostly urban one at that. Yet the first acknowledged line-of-duty police death in this ongoing war took place on the waning cusp of the 19th century. And it didn't happen on the mean streets of New York, Chicago or Los Angeles, but in a sleepy little country village along the Platte River in Missouri.

John Henry Dillingham, like many early Missourians, was a native of Kentucky. Born in Richmond, Madison County, on September 29, 1853, Dillingham was an infant when his family migrated west and settled near Mosby, in Clay County, Missouri. About four years later, the Dillinghams moved to Platte County and established a farm about five miles east of Platte City, the county seat. It was here that John Dillingham, as a later biographer put it, "grew up to manhood," and became "noted for physical and moral courage, and a readiness to engage in any undertaking promising adventure."

In the mid 1870s, Dillingham went to Nevada in charge of some livestock for his father. The lure of the west took strong hold on the adventurous young man and he "remained in the west for some time." He reportedly worked a brief stint as a lawman in Butte, Montana, before returning to Platte County – and farming – in the late 1870s. On August 31, 1876, John married Anna Oldham at the Oldham family's home in Platte County. The couple had six children over the years. The oldest, Henry Lee Dillingham, born in 1877, would later find distinction of his own, and would figure significantly in the tragedy that claimed his father's life.

In the late 1880s Anna's health began to fail and the family packed up and moved to the drier, healthier climate of Colorado. They returned after only a couple of years, and on January 20, 1891, Anna Dillingham died in Platte City. A single father now, John went into the livery business in Platte City, and in mid-1892 was reported to be building his family "a two-story handsome frame [house]" in the city. During this time, he was appointed Platte City Marshal, a post he would hold until 1896.

Along with his business and his marshal's duties, Dillingham took a commission as a deputy sheriff serving under Platte County's Sheriff James Synnamon. He proved an able, tireless deputy, once chasing a horse thief into the treacherous Indian Territory, "stopping only to eat, snatch a few hours sleep, and change horses." He brought back his man and when the outlaw broke jail and fled the area, Dillingham dogged him to Vicksburg, Mississippi, and recaptured him. There were no jail breaks this time – the thief was convicted in a Missouri court and sent to prison for his crime.

Having established himself as a staunch member of his community – a public servant, businessman and member of the local Odd Fellows lodge – Dillingham decided to seek public office. His first effort was a disappointment; in the Democratic primary on June 18, 1892, he finished a distant third behind Oscar Berry as nominee for Platte County Sheriff. There were apparently no hard feelings on either's part; Dillingham continued as a deputy sheriff when Sheriff Berry took office in January 1893.

John Dillingham
(Author's Collection)

In March of 1893, Dillingham remarried, to Catherine (Kate) Nash at Platte City. He was not to be deterred in office-seeking for long; in March of 1896, he resigned as city marshal to put his full efforts into another campaign for the sheriff's star. It was a shrewd move – he won the party's nomination by a five-to-one margin and in November was elected over his opponent, George Doppler, by a three-to-one margin.

The very next month the new sheriff found himself in the middle of an interstate jurisdictional and political dispute. Platte County is situated in far northwest Missouri, just across the Missouri River from Leavenworth, Kansas. On December 17, a shooting took place on Stiger's Island, a disputed bit of land smack in the Missouri River. There a black man named Frank Garrison shot a German immigrant named Frank Ulrich. Jurisdiction over the crime was unclear; both Missouri and Kansas claimed the island, and the issue was awaiting adjudication in the courts. Meanwhile, Ulrich lay hospitalized in Leavenworth, Kansas, and Garrison sat lodged in the Leavenworth County jail. The day after the shooting, Sheriff Dillingham crossed the state line with a warrant for Garrison's arrest on the shooting charge.

The Kansas authorities smelled a rat. "It is claimed," reported the *Kansas City Daily Journal*, "that the Missouri warrant...is nothing more or less than an effort to have, through the trial of Garrison, the courts pass on the legal situation of this island, in its decision as to the question of jurisdiction, thus saving the costs incident to a civil procedure." If that weren't enough, there were fears circulating, stoked by the press, that Garrison was in danger of being lynched the moment he returned to Missouri soil. The *Kansas City Journal* printed Garrison's friends' claim that there was a "prearranged plan whereby a mob was to have taken him from Sheriff Dillingham once he was across the river, and make short work of him."

At the Leavenworth jail, Dillingham had a hot debate with the Leavenworth County Sheriff, Peter Everhardy. "Much feeling was exhibited by each of the sheriffs," the *Kansas City Journal* wrote, "but matters were quieted down by Garrison who demanded requisition papers. This necessarily shut the Platte County officer out."

Whatever he thought of the threats, Garrison apparently preferred to take his chances in Kansas, a notoriously lenient state. While jurisdiction and extradition were being argued by the lawmen and the local court, matters took a serious turn. Ulrich died on December 20, and Frank Garrison was now facing a murder charge. The same day, Dillingham (exasperated with the lack of cooperation in Leavenworth County) set off for Topeka to plead his case before Kansas Governor Edmund Morrill.

Though Kansas would ultimately prevail in the land dispute, Dillingham won the debate over jurisdiction in the Garrison case and was allowed to return to Missouri with his prisoner. Dire predictions of angry mobs notwithstanding, Garrison was soon safely housed in the Platte Country jail. Safely, but apparently not securely. Months later, in the early hours of September 21, 1897, Garrison and four other prisoners escaped – possibly with outside help – by removing a stone from the jail's outer wall. The *Kansas City Journal* complained "the Platte City jail is a poor one, and prisoners are constantly escaping from it."

One of Garrison's fellow escapees was a particularly heinous offender: James Geer, who had been awaiting trial in the rape of a 10-year-old girl. Dillingham announced a $25 reward for capture of any of the fugitives, and he tracked them with his personally-owned pack of bloodhounds. Garrison and Geer weren't at large for long. Dillingham and Detective Brady of the Kansas City, Missouri, police recaptured them near Holliday, in Monroe County, on the 24th. Both were armed but surrendered peacefully and were returned to the calaboose. Garrison's conviction would ultimately be overturned; Geer was hanged at Liberty, Missouri, in December.

In late November 1898, Dillingham became involved in another sensational murder case that threatened to end in a lynching. William Foley had been convicted in Clay County, Missouri, of the murders of his mother and sister. His case had been appealed to the Missouri Supreme Court, the decision reversed, and a new trial ordered. This did not sit well with some of Clay County's more hardnosed law-and-order citizens. After several failed attempts by mobs bent on lynching Foley, he'd been moved to the Kansas City jail for his own safety. In mid-November, Clay County Judge Broaddus, "after being convinced that Foley's life would be worth less than a postage stamp if he were required to appear in court at Liberty," granted a change of venue to Platte County. His choice of Platte pleased neither Foley nor his attorney, both of whom feared that the Clay County mobs would still target Foley there. But Sheriff Dillingham, who traveled alone to Kansas City to take charge of the prisoner, did his best to calm their fears. "We don't love Foley any more than our Clay County friends do," Dillingham told the *Kansas City Journal*, "but he is our prisoner and we shall protect him." The sheriff guaranteed to keep "a strong guard about the jail," including his pack of bloodhounds. Dillingham was as good as his word. He escorted Foley to the Platte County jail, traveling by train and rented wagon without incident. The following February, Foley was acquitted of his mother's murder, and although the citizens were "very indignant over the verdict," there were no vigilante actions. While Foley remained safely housed in Platte County's jail awaiting a new trial in his sister's murder, the *Journal* highly praised Platte County Judge Alonso D. Burnes for his impartial handling of the case, and Sheriff Dillingham and his deputies for the "skillful manner in which they handled the large crowds."

The first week of December 1899, Sheriff Dillingham was about to officiate at his first execution – the hanging of Charles Grant, who'd been convicted of murdering his wife. Having no practical experience in such matters, Dillingham again visited the Kansas City jail, this time "in search of pointers upon the most expeditious and scientific way to hang a man." Armed with the necessary knowledge, he returned to Platte City and began work on a tall fence around the scaffold, as required by a new state statute. A Hope County newspaper railed on this point, condemning the "sickly sentimental laws made by an idiotic legislature," and called for executions to return to public view to "terrify by example persons from breaking the laws of the land." It was no matter; on December 5, Governor Lawrence Vest "Lon" Stephens granted the condemned man a thirty-day stay of execution. His sentence was evidently commuted later on, for there is no record that Grant was ever hanged.

Sleepy little Farley, Missouri, was one of those quiet burgs where nothing much goes on. But folks who say "it can't happen here" are deluding themselves. Bad business knows no geographical boundaries; it can occur anywhere, at any time. Every smart lawman knows that, and Sheriff John Dillingham was a smart lawman. Still, even a man of his experience could not have foreseen just how bad things would get in Farley on August 20, 1900.

Situated just north of the junction of the Platte and Missouri Rivers, and just across the Big Muddy from Leavenworth, Kansas, Farley was little more than a cluster of small farms and a dusty little main street with a general store next to a Masonic Lodge – both of which would factor in the day's events. Farley also had a doctor: Sterling Price Harrington. Born August 22, 1864, "Sturley" Harrington was a native son whose family had come to Missouri just a handful of years behind Lewis and Clark. His grandfather had been one of the first to settle this section of Platte County. The young

Sterling Price "Sturley" Harrington came from an old and respected Missouri family, and was reputed to be a competent doctor when he wasn't drinking. (*Author's Collection*)

Harrington took his medical training in Kansas City in the 1880s, then returned to Platte County to hang out his shingle. The new doctor and his brother Luther became "zealous members" of the Masonic Lodge at Farley. In May 1888, Sturley married Mary Edna Wallace, daughter of a respectable Platte County family. He was said to be a capable enough doctor. But he had a volatile temper and a drinking problem to boot, which no doubt affected his medical practice, and certainly affected his home life.

"He was kind and considerate enough when sober," the *Kansas City Star* later wrote of Harrington, "but when drinking his entire manner changed. He became a fiend."

The good doctor's condition became so problematic that in 1897 he went to Kansas City for the "Keeley Cure," a celebrated – and highly suspect – addiction treatment of the era. Like many others who had sought to get clean and sober the Keeley way, Harrington failed. Soon after returning to Farley he was back at the bottle. Not only that, but he'd returned with a worse problem not uncommon among Keeley patients – he was addicted to cocaine.

His demons soon began to take complete charge. There was "common talk" around town that Mary Harrington lived in constant fear of the doctor's violent outbursts. The year after taking "the cure," Harrington attacked Herman Meyer, the town's postmaster and a brother Mason, with a knife. Though apparently not charged, Harrington was summarily ejected from the Lodge, and it may have been in part his grievance over this that led to his final, bloody rampage. The trouble had started days before; the previous Thursday, Sturley has reportedly been "on a spree."

On Saturday, August 18, neighbors who heard screaming and shouting coming from the Harrington home thought little of it. It was not an unusual occurrence. Mary Harrington would later claim that her husband had tried to kill her.

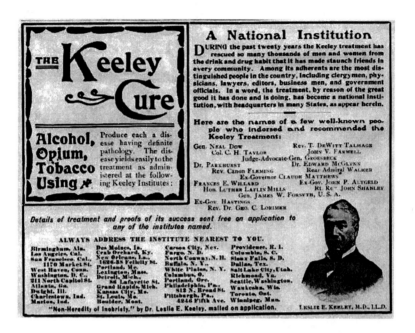

Sturley Harrington's attempt to overcome his alcoholism by taking the popular and controversial Keeley Cure was a tragic failure. *(Author's Collection)*

At 5:30 Sunday morning a neighbor saw Mary and ten-year-old daughter Maude in the family's back yard, and heard Mrs. Harrington tell Maude to go to her uncle's house for a "pitcher of milk." As soon as the girl was out of sight, Mary fled to another neighbor's house, where she hid in the attic. She remained there "in spite of all pleadings of neighbors and friends," and despite the stifling temperatures of a record heat wave, until well after dark. Under the safe cover of night, she made her way to her mother's house, about two miles away. Mary Wallace was a widow of 62. Her husband William had died in the last year, and she lived with her son Robert. After consulting with her mother, Mary had her brother drive her in a buggy to Leavenworth, Kansas, about six miles away. She spent the night in the train depot, and early Monday morning she rode the train back over the state line to Platte City, Missouri, about twelve miles northeast of Leavenworth.

There she would see Sheriff Dillingham, who some sources say was a cousin, and swear out a complaint against her husband.

Harrington, meanwhile, had apparently been inside the family's home the entire day Sunday. Whether he'd been on a bender or merely brooding, no one knew. Neighbors saw him emerge around 5 a.m. on Monday the 20th and hitch up a light wagon. He then walked to a hill behind his home, "mounted a haystack" and stood staring in the direction of Mary Wallace's house. After a time, he returned to the house and called to his daughter Maude. The two of them boarded the wagon and headed down "the hot, dusty road to the lane leading to his mother-in-law's house." It was just after 6 a.m. Harrington was carrying two or three revolvers, and one newspaper would later speculate that he'd set out "to find his wife to kill her." Another said simply that, "Crazed by whiskey and cocaine, with murder in his heart, Dr. Sterling Price Harrington started on a four hours [sic] career of crime." Oddly, most who saw him early that morning said he didn't appear drunk. Although the *Moberly Weekly Monitor* acknowledged Harrington was "under the influence of some powerful drug, probably cocaine," it observed that "never a man in his sanest moments acted with more coolness and presence of mind."

When they arrived at Mary Wallace's house, Harrington left little Maude in the wagon holding the reins. Finding the front door locked, he walked around the house to the kitchen door, out of his daughter's view. He found Mary Wallace sitting at the kitchen table eating her breakfast. No one knows exactly what took place when Harrington confronted his mother-in-law; he was most likely looking for information about his wife's whereabouts. Maude soon heard three gunshots in quick succession. Harrington walked out, locking the kitchen door behind him, and casually returned to the wagon. As they drove away, Maude asked her father "Papa, did you kill Grandma?" He replied with callous frankness, "Yes, I killed her."

Most children would have been horrified, but the girl was evidently by now so numbed to violence that nothing her father did surprised her. "Maude showed no horror," the *Kansas City Star* wrote. She rather "received the news in silence and with absolute indifference. She had grown up to the age of ten years in an atmosphere of daily threats of her father against her mother so that the news made no impression on her."

Maude asked where they were now going. Harrington answered, "to Uncle Jim's," and pointed the wagon east. James Wallace, Mary Wallace's brother, lived about half a mile away. When they pulled up at the house, Harrington again left Maude in the wagon. In the front yard stood Sarah Wallace, Jim's wife, and their daughter, Emma Farley. Emma's husband John and a teenage granddaughter named May were also in the yard. Harrington gave them a pleasant greeting, and his cheerful demeanor apparently gave none of the group any inkling of his dark plans. Harrington asked Sarah Wallace, "Where is Uncle Jim?" She replied that he was "around the house somewhere." Harrington walked around to the rear of the house and he found Jim Wallace, a cheery Irishman in his mid 70s, working on a buggy wheel. Accounts of precisely what occurred differ. One said that Harrington demanded to know where Mary was and "became abusive" when Wallace claimed ignorance. Another says Harrington called a friendly good morning to the old man, and when he turned from his work, shot him. In any case, the shooting was witnessed by John Farley and the girl May, who both saw Harrington fire three shots. The first hit Wallace in the mouth, the second and third passed through his torso. He slumped against the wheel he'd been repairing. As Harrington calmly walked away, pocketing his revolver, Emma Farley ran to her father's side. "Why did he do it?" she cried, and Wallace managed to say, "I don't know." The words were his last; he died as Sterling and Maude Harrington drove away. Having heard the shots, the impassive little girl asked, "Did you kill Uncle Jim, too, Papa?" Harrington answered, "Yes, I killed him too."

From the Wallace house, Harrington drove across the Missouri River to Leavenworth, Kansas. Whether he was looking for Mary here is unclear; he rolled into Leavenworth about 8 a.m. and drove to a hardware store owned by William Carney. One account says he visited at least two saloons first. This may well be, for in contrast to earlier descriptions, at Carney's Harrington was said to be "under the influence of liquor though he did not seem excited." Inebriated or not, Carney sold the doctor a .41 caliber Winchester rifle, a couple of boxes of rifle cartridges and a hundred .38 caliber pistol cartridges. Harrington explained the ammunition by telling Carney, "I have an order for the cartridges in the store in Farley and as I am going home, I might as well take them."

As Harrington stashed his purchases in the wagon and climbed back aboard, Maude asked where they were headed now. Her father's answer was simple: "Home."

While the Harringtons were crossing back over the state line, James Wallace's family had sent word of his shooting throughout Farley. A young neighbor named Charley Oberdick was sent to Mary Wallace's house to check on her welfare. He broke in the kitchen door and confronted a gruesome sight – Mary Wallace lay sprawled on the kitchen floor, dead. She'd been shot in the mouth in the same way her brother had, the bullet lodging in the back of her neck. Another had entered under her right arm, apparently as she raised it in defense, and had passed through her body "so that it could be felt beneath the skin on the left side." Harrington's other shot had gone wild. Oberdick ran back to Jim Wallace's house and gave the family the grim news. There was no telephone or telegraph in Farley, so a messenger set off to East Leavenworth, Missouri, about four miles north, to wire Sheriff Dillingham in Platte City.

Upon getting the news, Dillingham immediately set off for Farley with three deputies: Joseph Elgin, Eli Berry, and the sheriff's eldest son, Henry – himself a former Platte City marshal. "In the meantime," wrote the *Kansas City Star*, "Harrington and little Maude were on their way home. When they arrived at Farley, although the entire town knew of the double murder, no hand was raised to arrest him." The citizens of Farley knew all too well what Harrington was like on a "spree," let alone on a shooting spree.

Harrington drove up the town's main street and stopped in front of the general store owned by his neighbor, William Wiehe. Once again leaving Maude with the wagon, Harrington stepped inside. He walked past the clerk, Daniel Cannon, and went to the back of the store where Wiehe sat talking to two local men, John Polk and H.H. Moss. The atmosphere was surely charged; by now everyone in town knew what Harrington had done. It must have been especially tense for Dan Cannon. He was a boarder at James and Sarah Wallace's house, and he and Jim had been Sterling Harrington's brothers in the Masonic lodge. It was said that the doctor blamed them both for his ouster and had threatened to "clean out every Mason in Platte County."

If there was tension, no one let it show. Perhaps thinking ahead to escape, Harrington asked Wiehe to give him all the money he had. The old man calmly refused. Harrington made the same request of Moss and Polk, and they also refused. Harrington was unfazed. He laughed, said, "That's all right," and walked back to the counter where Cannon stood. "Dan," he asked, "how much money do you have in the store?" Cannon replied that he had three dollars (some accounts say four). Not much, but Harrington had come for money and didn't intend to leave without it. "Give it to me," he told Cannon, "and I'll pay you back out of the wheat when it is sold." Cannon replied that the money was Wiehe's and he couldn't let him have it. Now Harrington became testy. "Yes you can," he insisted, "for I will pay it back." When he was refused again, Harrington whipped out a pistol, shoved the muzzle in Cannon's face, and demanded the money. Cannon handed it over. As Harrington stepped back, stuffing the bills into his pocket, he turned slightly away and lowered his gun. "This was the opportunity Cannon had been looking for," said the *Kansas City Star*. "He drew his pistol from beneath the counter and fired. He missed."

A furious volley of gunfire ensued. Harrington and Cannon, standing only a few feet apart, emptied pistols at each other. The men in back ducked for cover. A farmer named James Young was grazed on the arm, and another bullet perforated his shirt. Despite the close range, neither combatant was injured. Cannon's last round struck Sterling's pistol, "shattering it and putting it out of action." The quick-thinking clerk dropped behind the counter and gasped out, "I'm shot," hoping the doctor would be fooled. It worked; Harrington tossed his ruined pistol aside, drew another, and headed for the door. He was unaware that while he was shooting up Wiehe's store, Sheriff Dillingham and party had arrived at Farley, been alerted, and at that moment were making their way toward the store.

Two seconds one way or the other and this incident might have ended very differently. As it was, the sheriff and the doctor arrived at opposite sides of the store's doorway at the same moment. The advantage was Harrington's – he was primed, gun in hand, and driven by both cocaine and adrenalin. Dillingham, pupils constricted by the bright morning sunshine, was staring through a screen door into the subdued light of Wiehe's store. The fact that he got off a shot at all is remarkable. As the *Star* reported it, "instantly the two revolvers came up and were fired with almost a simultaneous report. Dillingham fell on the store's porch with a bullet between the eyes." The round actually struck him in mid-forehead. "His shot," the *Star* said of Dillingham, "had just grazed the doctor's forehead and cut his hat brim." The sheriff's bullet lodged in the store's ceiling.

Harrington's shot took deadly effect; John Dillingham died almost instantly. His body had fallen blocking the doorway, so that Harrington had to step over him in leaving the store. He leaped from the porch and made for his wagon. Henry Dillingham, standing close by and no doubt reeling from the shock of seeing his father gunned down, reacted in an instant. He leveled his pistol at the fleeing killer and fired three times. "Every shot took effect," said the *Star*. "One passed through the heart, another entered the left side between the fourth and fifth rib, and the third entered the left breast. He fell in the dusty road dead." Sterling Harrington's brief and bloody reign of terror was ended.

Only now did his daughter show any emotion. "The child Maude who had been sitting in the buggy for four hours and had all but seen two persons murdered," the *Star* wrote, "now lost her indifference. She dropped the reins and scrambled to the ground. Swiftly she ran to her father's side and throwing herself on his body sobbed and wept and cried Papa, Papa, Papa." Hers were the only tears shed for Sterling Price Harrington in the town of Farley that day.

Dr. Stewart McKee, who'd been summoned from Leavenworth, arrived to find four dead bodies awaiting him. Harrington's body was turned over to the Platte County Coroner. The late doctor was found to be carrying three revolvers and over 200 rounds of ammunition. A "Two Thousand Mile Transportation Book" was in his pocket. It seemed Harrington had some vague plans of escaping after carrying out his bloody work, which may account for his taking his young daughter along on his grim errands. Dillingham's body was taken to Leavenworth under care of Dr. McKee.

Though nobody but Maude shed tears for Harrington (likely mingled with some sense of relief), John Dillingham was truly missed. "No death was more widely and sincerely mourned in Platte County," said Missouri journalist Walter Williams. He offered a fitting eulogy of Dillingham when he wrote, "John H. Dillingham was a man without fear and without reproach, and his courage was tempered by the kindliness and tenderness which have so often marked heroic natures." As a man, and as a lawman, John Dillingham had left large boots to fill.

Governor Stephens appointed Henry Dillingham a week later to serve out his father's term as Platte County Sheriff, even though he was only twenty-two. Henry performed ably until his term expired, then he made a career change and became, in an odd touch of irony, a pharmacist. He married Mary June Cockrill in 1901, and the couple had two daughters. Henry operated a drug store until 1909, then turned to farming and real estate. He became an active civic leader, serving as a Platte City Councilman, Chairman of the Platte County Fair Association, Chairman of the Platte County Democratic Committee, and represented the 4th Congressional District in state committee. In the late 1930s, owing to Henry's public service record – and possibly in part to his actions on August 20, 1900 – President Franklin D. Roosevelt appointed him as U.S. Marshal for the Western District of Missouri.

Henry Dillingham lived until 1948; Maude Harrington lived until 1973. What different memories each must have had of that long-past summer day. John Dillingham is buried in the Platte City cemetery where Dillinghams long before and after him were laid to rest. Sterling Price Harrington was buried in the Farley Cemetery. Both lie under stately and oddly similar stone markers.

Harrington's grave marker contains something Dillingham's does not. A simple inscription below the dates reads, "Gone but not forgotten." It is a sentiment that might be taken different ways. Dillingham has an unambiguous tribute of his own. A historical marker near the store – which still stands – where he had his fateful encounter reads:

"This marker is dedicated to the memory of John H. Dillingham, Sheriff of Platte County Missouri from 1896 to 1900 – First law enforcement officer killed in the line of duty in Platte County. Killed on this spot on August 20, 1900, by Dr. Sterling Price Harrington when Sheriff Dillingham attempted to arrest him for the murders of James Wallace and Mary Wallace, both of whom were killed by Dr. Harrington earlier on August 20, 1900. Deputy Sheriff Henry Dillingham, Sheriff Dillingham's son, returned Dr. Harrington's gunfire and killed Dr. Harrington, also on this spot. Dedicated by the

Dillingham and Farley families, descendants of John H. Dillingham and the Wallaces. Platte County Historical Society."

MAD DOCTOR KILLS MANY

Including His Wife's Relations and the County Sheriff.

WHISKY WAS THE CAUSE

Little Daughter Witnessed the Series of Tragedies.

EMBRACING THE FINALE

Which Was the Death of Her Father
at the Hands of the Dead
Sheriff's Son.

The *Wichita Daily Eagle* was one of many newspapers that publicly blamed Harrington's rampage on drink, drugs, or both. *(Author's Collection)*

Chapter 9: "...*the posse opened fire and a lively fusillade ensued.*"
      Special Agent David Frank Calhoun
      Atchison, Topeka and Santa Fe Railway Police
      (July 12, 1905)

Frank Calhoun wasn't looking to get involved. For one thing, it was his birthday. For another, he had been traveling all day, was tired, and likely all he wanted was to get a hotel room and maybe a meal, then turn in for the night. The Baird House wasn't the best hotel in Kansas, but it was supposed to be best in Cedar Vale; it was described as "exceedingly popular among commercial travelers and especially known as a good place to Sunday in." It was Tuesday, but Calhoun turned his steps in that direction. As he passed through the Santa Fe train yard, two fellows walking through caught his attention. They just didn't look right. He couldn't have explained why. But Frank Calhoun had been a lawman long enough to know one thing: when you felt that vague, itchy sensation at the back of your brain that said all was not as it should be, you'd better pay attention. That sixth sense was never wrong. He had nothing on the men at the moment, no reason to ask their business. But he would keep eyes and ears open while he was in town. Odds were good he'd be seeing those two birds again.

A common presence in towns throughout the country in the latter 19th century, and early part of the 20th, was the railroad detective. This was particularly true in the West, where trains ran though long, lonely stretches of unsettled, or only partly settled, country. Towns were often few and far between and the trains and their passengers tempting targets and easy pickings for the criminal class. Though railway lines were private corporations, like banks and express companies they were crucial to keeping America operating. As such, they were allowed by law to form special police organizations to look after their interests – to prevent, intervene in, and investigate crimes against the railroads and their patrons. Such men, known variously as "special agents" or "detectives," were vested with specific police powers in the scope of their jobs, and often had broadened authority by way of commissions as local officers, deputy sheriffs, or deputy federal marshals in the jurisdictions they worked.

David Frank Calhoun was one of these men – a detective in the employ of the Atchinson, Topeka & Santa Fe Railroad. Exactly how long he had worked for the Santa Fe is uncertain. He may have first done a brief stretch working for the famed Thiel's Detective Agency. Prior to that, back in 1899 he was the city marshal in Galena, Kansas. Many current references to Frank Calhoun, even his listing on the National Law Enforcement Memorial in Washington, D.C., refer to him as "C.S. Calhoun." The error seems to trace back to Associated Press dispatches reporting his death, and probably owes much to the poor sound quality of early telephones. To a 1905 newsroom operative speaking long distance to a field reporter on one of those squawk boxes, "D. F. Calhoun" could easily have come across as "C. S. Calhoun."

Frank Calhoun was born July 11, 1873, in Norwood, Missouri. He was the second of six children born to James Franklin Calhoun and Lucinda Hellums Calhoun. Very little record exists of Frank's early life; he was raised in Wright County, Missouri, and by 1899 he was married to Hattie Colson and had two young daughters, Avis and Grace. At that time he was serving as the city marshal in Galena, a little lead mining town in the southeastern corner of Kansas, near both the Missouri and the Oklahoma Territory borders.

Just days after his 26th birthday, Marshal Calhoun became involved in the most significant event of his time in Galena, the murder of John E. Purvis. In the predawn hours of July 13, 1899, a local black man named Mose Locke, who was described as "a cripple," came into Galena, on foot and distraught. He reported that

Purvis, a local white farmer who'd hired Locke to travel with him into the Indian Territory, had been shot and killed at their campsite near Shoal Creek, about three miles south. Locke said he'd been awakened a couple of hours earlier by gunshots and groans. He had found Purvis shot and dying, and "two negroes in their camp." The two men, Locke claimed, had robbed Purvis of $12 and relieved Locke of $1.50 while he slept. The robbers cut his and Purvis' horses loose then chased him, Locke said, and he'd only escaped murder himself by fleeing into the brush, then hiding until the bandits left. While Locke was telling this story, the two errant horses wandered into Galena as though on cue, and were found roaming the streets. Something about Locke's story just didn't wash.

A party of city and Cherokee County lawmen, including Sheriff Oliver Sparks and Marshal Calhoun, rode out to Shoal Creek to investigate. They found Purvis stone dead, lying face down with two bullets in his head and one in his abdomen. A fourth had been fired into his back as he lay prone, exited near his heart, and was found embedded in the soft earth beneath his body. Skeptical of Locke's account, the officers arrested him and lodged him in the jail in Galena. He was freed briefly a couple of days later after a coroner's jury attributed Purvis' death to person or persons unknown, but the local officers rearrested him on the 17th and were able to quickly get to the bottom of things. The *Kansas City Star* reported that "Sheriff Sparks, M.F. Parker, City Marshal Frank Calhoun and others, by promising Locke protection and questioning him, secured a confession that he and another man murdered Purvis for his money." Locke admitted conspiring with two friends, Will Carey and his 17-year-old son, J. W. Carey, to rob Purvis.

At a prearranged hour, Locke told the lawmen, the Careys had ridden into their camp. Finding Purvis still awake, Carey had summarily shot him, continuing to fire into him after he fell. They robbed Purvis, then all three mounted and rode north, separating just outside Galena where Locke dismounted and walked into town. Carey released the two horses to bolster Locke's claims. With Locke's confession in hand the officers arrested Will and J.W. Carey for murder, and at a preliminary hearing in Galena on the 29th, all three were bound over for trial.

Five years later, Frank Calhoun was back in Missouri, living near Kansas City, and he and Hattie had a two-year-old son, Theodore. Now employed by the Atchison, Topeka and Santa Fe Railway, Frank was part of a team of detectives sent in mid-May 1905, to Lyon County, Kansas. They were investigating a train derailment; someone had broken into a tool house along the Santa Fe line a few miles from Emporia. Using tools from the shed, they had pulled up fishplates and spikes at a sharp curve in the track, and when Santa Fe Train #17 came chuffing through at about 2:30 a.m. on May 14, the entire eight car train, with between fifty and sixty people onboard, was "put in the ditch."

Emporia's city marshal quickly arrested two vagrants on suspicion after a young boy claimed he'd seen them in the area and heard them discussing how to burglarize the tool house. The day after the wreck the *Emporia Gazette* reported that the two suspects were "being 'sweated out' by Marshal Francis and the three Santa Fe Detectives, Germaine, Burge and Calhoun." H.H. Germaine, "the king bee in the swarm of detectives," was the ATSF's chief special agent; along with Joe Burge and Frank Calhoun he'd been charged with getting to the bottom of the derailment.

Six passengers had been injured in the wreck, two very badly, and several others were reported missing but were later accounted for. There had been earlier attempts to derail the same train, and the detectives believed all were the work of the same person or persons. Superintendent J.E. Hurley of the Santa Fe was quick to publicize his theory that a vengeful former employee, and not strikers, had caused the wreck, but the detectives were not so certain. The railroad offered a $5,000 reward for information leading to the guilty party, and

Governor Edward Hoch bumped it up by $300 – the maximum allowed by Kansas law. After a couple of newspaper editorials caterwauling about conflicts of interest, Germaine gave the *Gazette* a statement clarifying that he and his fellow detectives were by ATSF policy ineligible for either reward. Beyond that disclaimer, the Santa Fe men talked little to the press. Calhoun, in particular, the *Gazette* later wrote, had "a detectives [sic] talent for keeping 'mum' about what he found out."

In the days after the derailment, Marshal Francis and the detectives received significant help from Lyon County Sheriff Stephen Hinshaw. The sheriff appointed eleven new deputies, costs paid by the Santa Fe, to guard the wreck site from looters and nosy gawkers. He also found some promising clues – wagon tracks and a woman's shoeprints – at the scene. Although the *Gazette* reported hopefully that "the detectives are close upon a clew [sic] implicating an Emporia woman," and although the officers arrested and questioned several other tramps, the case was destined to go unsolved.

PROBLEM OF SANTA FE WRECK UNSOLVED

No Definite Clew to Perpetrators of Yesterday's Crime---- Two Tramps Arrested and Held on Suspic- ion---One Death Has Resulted.

Frank Calhoun was part of a team of detectives investigating a deliberate train derailment near Emporia, Kansas. The crime was destined to remain unsolved. *(Author's Collection)*

In mid-December someone using the same m.o. derailed #17 again. This time there were two fatalities – the express messenger and the engineer. By January 1906, the rewards were still unpaid. By that point, sadly, Frank Calhoun would be six months beyond concern with such matters.

When the *Emporia Gazette* remarked on Detective Calhoun's taciturn work demeanor it also went on to praise him, saying that he was "well liked by the officers and was always polite and congenial." It's peculiar how different two men, born and raised in similar circumstances, can turn out to be. William Chadburn, born just a couple of years before Calhoun, grew up in Sedan, Kansas, about forty miles west of Coffeyville. Like Calhoun's Missouri hometown, Sedan was a small town in the central part of its state. Both men were the sons of Civil War veterans; Calhoun's father had served in the Missouri infantry, Chadburn's in the Kansas cavalry. Both men's fathers were farmers, and they were each born in the midst of several siblings. Both worked, at various times, on either side of the Kansas/Missouri border, though their vocations were polar opposites. While Calhoun was a detective, Will Chadburn was a desperado.

The earliest newspaper mention of Chadburn was in the June 1, 1881, edition of the *Sedan Times*, when he was about ten years old. A brief paragraph mentioned that "Willie" Chadburn was bitten by a copperhead while picking strawberries. Could the snake have known what sort of fellow young Willie would grow up to be, it might have held back out of professional courtesy. For unless he was stealing the strawberries, this may have been the only time a newspaper ever mentioned Chadburn without connecting him to a crime. Like many Western outlaws, William Chadburn is a bit of a dark horse. Listed in the 1880s census as "John W. Chadburn," his age given as nine years, he's absent from his parents' home in subsequent state and federal census records. By 1893 he was said to be living in Caney, near Coffeyville (possibly with his younger brother Fred, a railroad brakeman). According to his hometown newspaper, Chadburn had "been an outlaw ever since he was big enough to hold up a gun and pull the trigger." He had held up J. K. Tulloss' store in Sedan in August of 1893, "following up," reported the *Sedan Lance*, "by several small hold-ups on the streets."

Chadburn began calling himself "Billy the Kid," seemingly determined to live up to the moniker, and then some. On the dodge shortly after his Sedan spree, he fell in with truly bad company and graduated from petty thefts and stick-ups to train robbery and murder. While skulking in the brush outside Coffeyville waiting for dark and a chance to sneak into town for supplies, Chadburn happened upon two kindred spirits who were also riding the owlhoot trail. Both of these men changed aliases probably more often than they changed socks; Chadburn – and the law – knew them as Hans (or Hanse) Hydrick and Claude Shephard. Even scummy water seeks its own level, and these three had certainly found theirs. Months earlier Hydrick had robbed and murdered a stable keeper in Arkansas.

Will Chadburn started his career of outlawry by holding up the J.K. Tulloss Store in Sedan, Kansas, where he grew up. *(Photo courtesy of the Kansas State Historical Society)*

He had been arrested and was jailed in Pine Bluff at the same time as Shephard, who was awaiting trial for burglary. The two broke jail together, blew a safe – apparently Shephard's specialty – at Buckner, Arkansas, then headed for the Indian Territory, and thence to Kansas, with visions of train robberies dancing in their heads. They sensed that Will Chadburn would make a welcome addition to their little gang, and so the three partnered up.

They weren't long in acting. In the early morning of September 3, all three boarded and halted a westbound St Louis & San Francisco Railway train near Mound Valley, in Labette County. The take wasn't much; they were unable to open the safe in the express car and had to resort to robbing the crew and passengers. The bandits relieved their victims of about $500 in cash and jewelry, plus a jug of Kentucky bourbon. They scuttled off into the darkness, but not before Shephard murdered the express messenger, Charles Chapman, in cold blood. Lawmen all over southern Kansas began rounding up known robbers and assorted riffraff; at least half a dozen men were hauled in under suspicion of being the Mound Valley robbers. Already a wanted man, owing to his Chautauqua County shenanigans, Will Chadburn by now certainly qualified as one of the "usual suspects." His brother Fred, "an honest, industrious young man" working for the Missouri Pacific rail line, was himself briefly caught up in the hunt for the killers. Whether a case of mistaken identity, or guilt by association, Fred found himself jailed in early October at Columbus, Kansas. He was released for lack of evidence days later when word reached Labette County that brother Will had been recognized and arrested by a constable in Dexter, Kansas. Witnesses positively identified William Chadburn, and lawmen on the case, including Wells Fargo's celebrated detective Fred Dodge, went to work convincing Will to peach on his cohorts. It took some persuasion, but the prospect of hanging for murder was a powerful lever. By early November, Chadburn had made his deal: in exchange for giving state's evidence

Two armed robbers later identified as William Chadburn and Ed Madigan interrupted a friendly poker game at the Brettun House in Winfield, Kansas. *(Author's Collection)*

salesmen reported the crime to the Winfield marshal, the two holdup men were in the wind. They might have gotten away clean had they not stopped over the next night in Cedar Vale, or at least had they not walked through the train yard and fallen under the gaze of a shrewd and sharp-eyed railroad detective who knew a jailbird when he spotted one.

When he reached the Baird House on the evening of July 11, Frank Calhoun probably wasn't thinking of the two shady characters he had seen. It was his birthday, he was far from home, and he no doubt had more pleasant things in mind, like a good night's sleep. It's not clear whether his stop in Cedar Vale had any connection with the Emporia train wreck investigation or was a stopover in a journey elsewhere. But here he was, and as he started to enter the hotel a conversation among a group of guests on the porch stopped him short. Louis Adams, the necktie drummer from Chicago, was regaling a couple of other men with the tale of having been robbed by two men in Winfield the day before.

Frank Calhoun was on his own business when he happened to spot the Winfield robbers on the sleepy streets of Cedar Vale. *(Author's Collection)*

Two men; that got Calhoun thinking. He asked Adams what the bandits looked like and was probably little surprised when the salesman described the two idlers he'd seen earlier.

Calhoun paid a visit to the town's marshal, Arthur Butler. He explained to Butler what Adams had told him, and what he himself had seen. He offered Butler his assistance, and within minutes the two lawmen, with Adams along to make identifications, were crisscrossing Cedar Vale in a buggy looking for Calhoun's two suspicious characters. They had no luck; by now, the men had probably left town. Night was coming on, so the three gave up their search, and Adams and Calhoun returned to the Baird House for supper and a welcome rest.

About 5:30 the next morning, Marshal Butler played a hunch. Near the Missouri-Pacific depot sat Cedar Vale's only "dollar-a-day" house, the Gladstone Hotel. If Calhoun's two skulkers were still around, that's where they'd be. Butler's hunch was correct; the desk clerk's description of two men who had arrived together the night before was a perfect fit.

Wisely electing to seek backup, Butler left the Gladstone, only to spot Chadburn and Madigan walking down the town's main street. Butler followed them at a distance for a couple of blocks, decided the men weren't leaving anytime soon, and hurried to the Baird House to rouse Calhoun and Adams. Both were more than willing to go along. While they dressed, Butler went to Schooley & Smith's livery stable to hire a rig. The only transport available was a covered two-seated surrey. Butler took it and told the livery man, William Thompson, "You come and go with me, I may want you to hold the team." Thompson and Butler arrived at the Baird House just as Calhoun and Adams came downstairs.

It was between 6:30 and 7:00 a.m. when they set off, going east toward the edge of town. Butler and Adams sat in back and Calhoun took the front seat on Thompson's left. Before they had gone two blocks, they spotted Chadburn and Madigan. The men were walking west along the right-hand side of the road, coming straight toward them. Adams recognized them at once as the Winfield robbers. If the two outlaws were suspicious of the men in the rig, they didn't show it. Adams said "Get a bee line on them now." But Calhoun, possibly feeling it safer to approach from behind, told Thompson to drive on by the men to a bend in the road, then turn around. Adams made a remark to Calhoun that he'd no doubt soon regret: "You are a dead one."

Thompson drove past the men, who showed no concern, and went about sixty yards to a point where the road curved away and dipped downhill. He brought the rig around and back up the hill. Just as they came within range, Chadburn spun around and drew his pistol. He snapped off two quick shots, backing toward a tall hedge at the roadside as he fired. Both rounds struck Calhoun, who was closest to him; one in the right knee and one in the left side. Calhoun called out, "I am shot," as both he and Butler returned fire. Both outlaws retreated behind the hedge, and Adams and Thompson took what cover they could. Chadburn and Madigan each emptied a pistol at the lawmen. Butler fired three rounds – two at Chadburn, and one at Madigan. Calhoun fired two or three times. Madigan and Butler were untouched; a round from the lawmen grazed Chadburn's forehead. Soon there was such a haze of smoke that it was difficult for both witnesses and combatants to see clearly. Between the gun smoke, the hedge, and the chaos, Chadburn and Madigan slipped away.

When the shooting stopped, Butler jumped from the surrey and told Thompson and Adams to take Calhoun to a doctor. The marshal intended to go after the outlaws, but was now afoot, alone, and out of range. Butler later said he did not see Madigan after firing at him, but that he saw Chadburn in the distance walking "leisurely down the road, apparently reloading his gun." Adams told Thompson to continue alone with Calhoun, while he ran to a neighboring house hoping to borrow "a shot gun or a revolver" and help Butler. Finding no suitable armament there, he abandoned the idea.

Thompson drove the wounded Calhoun to the office of Dr. John Ennis, who was, by mere coincidence, the local surgeon for the Santa Fe Railway. The doctor did his best, but Chadburn's second bullet had entered the left side of Calhoun's chest and traveled through to the other side without exiting. Within fifteen minutes of arriving at the doctor's office, David Frank Calhoun died.

His killers, meanwhile, had stolen two saddle horses from a livery barn and ridden off toward Hewins, about seven miles southeast, probably heading for the Indian Territory. Butler went to the L.C. Adam & Company general store to get a Winchester and ammunition, intending to form a posse. While there, he arranged to telephone Hewins and other nearby towns to warn them of the fugitives. He also notified Sheriff Henry Wilson in Sedan. Wilson also called Hewins and spoke to Eli Sanborn, a farmer and community leader there. A member of the Anti Horse Thief Association, Sanborn was evidently the closest thing to a deputy in the village. Wilson told him the gunmen were headed his way and asked that he "gather a crowd of men and try to capture them if possible."

While Sanborn was assembling a welcoming committee, Chadburn and Madigan were committing their last holdup. Along the road from Cedar Vale to Hewins, the pair met a man named Claypool, who ran a billiard hall in Cedar Vale. They forced him to give up his horse, leaving him one of the stolen mounts in trade. Around 8:15 a.m. the bandits rode into Hewins, as Sanborn was standing in the road recruiting W.E. Allen for the posse. Both Sanborn and Allen recognized the stolen horses, and knew these were the Cedar Vale killers. Sanborn ran home to fetch his Winchester, while Allen hurried up the street to the G.H. Mills hardware store, presumably to get a gun.

As Allen reached the doorstep, Chadburn and Madigan rode up and dismounted. One of the men (unknown which) asked Allen to sell him some cartridges. Allen replied that it wasn't his store, but they would surely sell the man some inside. The outlaw entered the store and returned seconds later, grumbling that the place was empty. He jerked his pistol and ordered Allen to come in and sell him cartridges. Seeing little sense in arguing, Allen led the man back inside.

As he returned with his Winchester, Sanborn saw the outlaws pull up at Mills' store. Loading on the run, he hurried a hundred yards up the block to Pope's store, where he had told the volunteers to assemble. Several men were waiting there; Jim Pope and Bob Akin, a railroad worker, had guns at the ready. Pope suggested they move out in front of the store, where they could cover the street. As they filed out, a young farmer named Walter Bennett worried that he had no gun. Sanborn said "Well, you are a better shot than I am; take this one," and gave Bennett his rifle.

Inside the hardware store, Allen had just fetched two boxes of .45 cartridges for the gunman, who insisted, "I am going to pay for all I get." Just then, G.H. Mills, the store's owner, entered. Whether from fear or curiosity, Allen stayed put, but he eagerly handed the customer off to Mills. At the man's request, Mills supplied him with a .41 caliber pistol and a box of cartridges for it. The outlaw browsed Mills' supply of long guns. He refused a Winchester rifle because it was only .22 caliber, and passed on a pump shotgun because Mills had no buckshot on hand.

The man handed over $7.30 for the pistol and three boxes of ammunition, then picked up his purchases and turned to go. At the door, he dropped one of the boxes and it burst open. As though time were no issue, the fellow crouched down and picked up the spilled cartridges. Followed by Mills and Allen, he walked outside to where his partner waited, loading his new pistol as he went. The gunman mounted and asked where the drugstore was, saying they wanted some whiskey. He was told there was none. Someone fetched him the next best thing, a bottle of Electric Bitters patent medicine, for which he also dutifully paid. The two fugitives each took a long pull at the bottle.

The posse was coming out of Pope's store at this moment. As Eli Sanborn handed Walter Bennett his Winchester, the outlaws pulled pistols and wheeled their horses toward Pope's. With a war whoop, they charged the townsmen.

It was a short battle. Pope stepped into the road as the others lined up on the porch. Allen took cover in Mills' store and only heard what followed. Brandishing a shotgun, Pope called out, "Hold up, boys!" The two horsemen answered with pistol shots. Pope stood his ground and repeated the order. The two men fired at him again, and then according to an A.P. dispatch, "the posse opened fire, and a lively fusillade ensued." As the free-for-all continued around the corner, "there was so much firing done," Sanborn said later, "and smoke between me and them I couldn't well see." When the black powder fog thinned, Sanborn saw that the townies had won the skirmish. Chadburn fell from his horse and quickly raised two empty hands. About 200 feet beyond, Madigan tumbled into the dust. Both horses were badly shot up and neither would survive. On the town's side, only two minor casualties were counted; Pope received a slight bullet wound in the foot and a Mrs. Malone, an elderly lady drawn out by curiosity, was shot in the leg.

As the Hewins posse faced down Frank Calhoun's killers, several other interested parties were bound for the area. Henry Powell, a Chautauqua County deputy sent by Sheriff Wilson from Elgin – ten miles southeast – arrived about the time the shooting stopped. Sheriff Wilson himself was in a buggy headed from Sedan to Cedar Vale to take charge of matters there. At the direction of ATSF Superintendent Hurley, a special train carrying a posse of railroad police was en route from Chanute, about eighty miles northeast. The railroad officers, eager to have a hand in capturing Calhoun's killers, were disappointed to find they had arrived too late.

Once the shooting was over, the posse moved in on the downed desperados. Madigan had hit the ground dead, with several buckshot wounds in his chest and right side. Chadburn had been hit multiple times in the abdomen, twice in the right hip, once in the leg, and had several "grazing shots" to the head. He was in sorry shape, but alive. As the posse closed on him somebody picked up his pistol from the road and handed it to Sanborn. Though he was down, Chadburn was determined to play "Billy the Kid" to the end. He "cursed his captors to a finish," reported the *Sedan Lance*, "and put in his time expressing his opinion of them and things in general in characteristic strong language." Chadburn gave the posse his name, and his dead partner's, but little else. Around this point Deputy Powell took official charge. He searched the dead man's pockets and found no identifying items, but came up with a handful of revolver and shotgun rounds. He took custody of both outlaws and drove them into Cedar Vale where Sheriff Wilson was waiting.

Dr. Ennis treated Chadburn's wounds. He performed postmortems on both Calhoun and Madigan and expected, apparently, to be performing one on Chadburn soon. Chadburn evidently thought so too; a news dispatch from Cedar Vale remarked that "he expressed a desire here to die."

But Chadburn's outlaw luck had not run out just yet. By the next day he was well enough to travel, in Sheriff Wilson's custody, back to Sedan. He admitted to Wilson that he and Madigan had robbed the poker players at Winfield. He said also that Madigan's family could be reached at Ponca City. He didn't need to tell the sheriff where to reach his own family; Chautauqua County lawmen were plenty familiar with Will Chadburn.

The concerned families were notified and the bodies of Calhoun and Madigan were held at a local undertaker's until a coroner's jury could assemble for the inquest that afternoon. After viewing the bodies, the jury adjourned until 10 a.m. on July 13. Madigan was planted in the potter's field, and Frank Calhoun's body was placed aboard a train and sent to his family in Missouri. While the area newspapers said little of the fallen lawman or the wife and children he left behind, they expressed great sympathy for the Chadburn and Madigan families. The "boys," wrote the *Sedan Lance*, "are sons of highly respected families and it would be impossible to express the degree of humiliation and sorrow that the relatives of both of the boys had been brought to suffer by their wayward conduct." There was probably much truth to this, though there was surely sorrow in the Calhoun home as well.

Madigan's mother and sister came to Cedar Vale to settle accounts; Mrs. Madigan paid Ed's funeral expenses and "all bills connected with the affair on Madigan's account," whatever those were. She expected, she said, to have his remains reburied later at Ponca City. She was also seeking, according to newspaper reports, "as much evidence as possible that would have a tendency to vindicate the Madigan boy." Ed was only 22, his mother claimed, and she believed that "bad whiskey and bad company" had led him astray; it was said that he and Chadburn had imbibed pretty freely at Winfield before the holdup and at any and every chance since. *In vino stultitia.* In her deluded grief, Mrs. Madigan overlooked the fact that Ed had landed himself in the calaboose at Guthrie two years earlier, well before he ever took up Will Chadburn's bad company.

There were no real surprises at the inquest on the 13th. Testimony came from witnesses and participants in both gunfights, at Cedar Vale and at Hewins. The verdict named William Chadburn the perpetrator of the "willful, unlawful, premeditated and felonious" killing of detective Frank Calhoun. The jury ruled Madigan's death justifiable, specifying that it came "by means of certain and divers guns in the hands of the posse of citizens to these jurors unknown, while resisting the attempt of said posse of citizens to arrest him." So much for Mrs. Madigan's innocent baby boy.

The final chapter of Frank Calhoun's death wasn't long in coming. By the day after the inquest, newspapers were reporting that Chadburn might recover from his wounds. There had been the usual threats of lynching back in Cedar Vale. Sheriff Wilson and several deputies had guarded against such efforts while Chadburn was under Dr. Ennis's care, and during the trip to Sedan. The vigil continued at the jail in Sedan but no attempts were made. It would soon be a moot point. On July 16, Chadburn's mother and sister visited him at the county jail in Sedan, saw to his comfort, then left for home on the noon train. At about 5:00 p.m. the self-styled badman "breathed his last," his hometown newspaper noted, "and the grave marks the end of his turbulent career."

BATTLE WITH DESPERADOES

Posse Composed of Citizens of the Little Village of Hewins Take Desperate Chances With Outlaws and Come Out on Top—Detective Killed at Cedar Vale.

The *Sedan Lance,* Chadburn's hometown newspaper, carried word of Frank Calhoun's death, and of the end of Chadburn's and Madigan's crime spree. *(Author's Collection)*

Chapter 10: *"Billy, just put up your gun for we are not going to have any trouble here."*
City Marshal John Morgan Rennix
New Castle, Colorado (November 25, 1910)

The story of John Rennix bears eerie resemblance to a highly-publicized modern-day case. In each, a rogue ex-lawman went on a deadly murder spree targeting both officers and civilians. In each, the killer left behind a written document in an effort to explain his motives and paint himself as a victim. Without giving too much away, the resolutions have their similarities as well. History truly has an odd, often unsettling way of repeating itself.

The little mile-high town built near the junction of Elk Creek and the Grand River (today named the Colorado) at the foot of some of Colorado's grandest buttes, was originally and unimaginatively called Grand Butte. Later, it was briefly known as Chapman. When over half a dozen rich veins of coal were found nearby, such clean and plentiful coal that one contemporary historian wrote, "it challenges the world for an equal," English coal miners who flocked to Garfield County for work proposed naming the burg after their homeland's prime coal town. So, with a minor American tweak, in 1888 Chapman became New Castle.

Owing to its large coal mining operations and its position along the routes of both the Denver & Rio Grande and the Colorado Midland railways, New Castle was in the catbird seat for nearly a decade. Coal ran the railroads, the railroads shipped the coal, and both provided jobs aplenty. By 1889, some fifty businesses – ten of them saloons – operated in town. Five years later there were twenty-two saloons and, on the outskirts of town, a red light district discreetly called the "peach orchard." By the early 1890s, four hundred miners toiled in the Consolidated Mine just west of town, on Ward's Peak, the Vulcan Mine across the Grand River, and several smaller operations. Unfortunately, the mines yielded a secondary product; methane gas. A series of mine explosions led to the closure of the major operations. One blast in 1899 caused a "coal seam" fire that still burns deep underground today.

New Castle was a thriving coal mining community before a series of disasters all but closed down the mines and left a fire burning deep underground that burns to this day. *(Photo courtesy of the Denver Public Library, Western History Collection [Call #8-12492])*

As mines shut down and miners moved on, the town's population dwindled from 2,500 in the mid-1890s to fewer than 800 by 1910. New Castle's economy base shifted to agriculture, particularly the growing of russet potatoes. When President Theodore Roosevelt stopped in New Castle on a bear hunting expedition in the spring of 1905, he left with – among other gifts – a basket of New Castle spuds.

William Griffith came to New Castle in the waning days of the coal boom. In the 1900 census he gave his occupation as "miner," although the *Denver Post* pegged him more accurately when it wrote that he was often "nothing but a common town loafer." Although his obituary claims he was born in Streeter, Illinois – probably because he claimed Illinois as his birthplace in the 1910 census – records indicate he was born in Pembrokeshire, Wales, in early 1874, and immigrated with his family to the United States in 1888. Griffith lived in Garfield County for most of his adult life and was known for two talents, only

one of which endeared him to the people there. He was a crackerjack baseball player who played catcher for clubs from Leadville, Aspen, Glenwood Springs and New Castle, helping his teams to many a victory. He was known throughout the region as "Colorow," after the fierce Ute chief who had inhabited the area until the late 1880s. It's uncertain whether Griffith earned the formidable nickname due to his skill on the diamond or thanks to his other defining talent: he was a world-class tippler, and mean as hell when on the juice. According to an obituary of sorts in the *Eagle Valley Enterprise*, Griffith "was considered a fairly good fellow when sober, but he became intoxicated frequently, and when under the influence of liquor was reckless and brutal."

William Griffith had himself been New Castle's marshal for a brief time. A boozing bully, his only real claim to fame was his skill on the baseball diamond. *(Author's Collection)*

In December of 1902, the local papers carried some happy Griffith news: his Christmas Day wedding to Inez Collins, in New Castle. It must have been a stormy marriage from the start, between Will Griffith's spotty employment and his bouts of drinking and hooliganism. During their time together he held one unlikely job. In 1905, "by some freak of circumstances," as the *Denver Post* described it, Griffith was appointed New Castle's marshal. Like most of his enterprises, it was short-lived. He was evidently often drunk on duty, and "when public indignation reached its height against him," the *Post* reported, New Castle Mayor George Norris took action. Finding the marshal in an especially tipsy state, the mayor demanded he surrender gun and badge. Griffith pulled out his pistol, but rather than handing it over, he shot Norris in the leg. The mayor must have had a forgiving nature, or maybe Griffith convinced him it was an accident, for although the incident left the mayor with a permanent limp, Griffith was never prosecuted. It marked, however, the end of his short, embarrassing career as a lawman. Five years later the marshal's badge would be worn by another transplant to Garfield County: John Morgan Rennix.

John Rennix came to Colorado from another coal mining region: Randolph County, West Virginia. Born August 7, 1867, he was the youngest son of George Washington Rennix and Patsy Chenoweth. Records of his early life are scanty, but John married Lieuvernia May Poe in Randolph County in August of 1889. John and May had four daughters; Ivy was born in 1890, Ruth in 1893, Thelma in 1896 and Myrtle in 1898. In late 1900, while Myrtle was yet an infant, the family moved to Colorado and settled in New Castle.

John and May Rennix quickly took to life in the new town. May served as secretary of the Ladies' Aid Society at the Congregational Church, while John worked at various jobs, from hauling freight to grading roads. The *New Castle Nonpareil* couldn't resist poking fun at the green fellow from West Virginia after he made a freighting trip to Aspen – some fifty miles away and 2,500 feet higher in altitude – in early May of 1901. "Rennix is still somewhat of a tenderfoot," it said, "but is learning fast and says the next time he leaves home for a trip like that, even if it is in July or August, he's going to take along all his winter clothes, and also rubber boots and umbrella." He had learned the hard way, the paper went on, "that Colorado has a different kind of a climate for every township."

Within a few months the newspapers would carry less light-hearted news of the Rennix family. On November 6, May Rennix gave birth to a son. On the 15th, little Johnnie Haskil Rennix died.

There must have been complications with the birth, for the following week the *Nonpareil* reported that "Mrs. J. M. Rennix who has been seriously ill, is reported as getting better," but two weeks after that wrote that May was "not so well, and in rather a

John Rennix graded roads and hauled freight up steep Colorado slopes before taking on the job of City Marshal in New Castle. *(Photo courtesy of the New Castle Historical Society)*

precarious condition." Three days before Christmas, May Rennix died at home. Suddenly, John was a single father raising four girls, ages three to eleven. He would marry again, but not until eight years later. Evaline Rightley Mead and John married in Glenwood Springs on July 14, 1909.

Meanwhile in July, 1905, *the New Castle Nonpareil* article, "The Glorious Fourth," detailed the town's "nice, quiet and modest little celebration" of the nation's birthday." Among the festivities covered, the paper made the following announcement: "The novelty race – walk a block, trot a block, run a block – was won by John Rennix." The *Aspen Democrat's* July 4 report on a baseball game between the Aspen and Glenwood Springs teams, which the latter won 10-2, praised the "particularly strong" play of the Glenwood catcher, "Colorow." It may have been the first occasion when both Rennix and Griffith made the papers. It was surely the best time. It would, unfortunately, not be the last.

Will Griffith's baseball exploits made news again in the summer of 1908. The June 13 *Aspen Democrat* looked forward to a game the following day between Aspen and Griffith's new team, New Castle. "Colorow and McMahon," the paper noted, "are especially proficient with the big stick and have broken many a Western Slope pitchers' [sic] heart." Griffith played as predicted, scoring New Castle's only runs on one of two doubles he hit that day. But in the end Aspen trounced New Castle for the first time in six years, with a score of 14-2. Had he been more astute, Griffith might have taken this as a sign that the sun was setting on his glory days.

Two years later Griffith was mostly living apart from his wife and running a saloon in New Castle on the ground floor of the Trimble building at Third and Main. A thirty-one-year-old widow named Leila McMichael ran a boarding establishment there, and Griffith roomed on the second floor. Theirs was not the normal landlord/tenant relationship; in the discretion of the times the local papers referred to McMichael as Griffith's "sweetheart."

In April of 1910, Griffith got into another drunken row, this time in his own saloon. A middle-aged man named John Pine ran afoul of Colorow – some reports said by trying to cadge free drinks – and was pummeled for his trouble. Griffith beat Pine so badly that he was rendered "a nearly helpless imbecile," and was hospitalized at the sanatorium in Glenwood Springs for months afterward. This time Griffith would not escape prosecution. He was held to answer for the aggravated assault on Pine and scheduled for trial at the Garfield County Court in Glenwood Springs.

A more temperate, sensible man, with a felony trial looming, might be on his best behavior. But Billy Griffith wasn't that sort. In October, Inez Griffith filed for divorce in Mesa County, alleging adultery, extreme cruelty and non-support. The adultery was

Griffith's carrying on with Leila McMichael. The non-support was a given. The cruelty stemmed from an incident in which Inez had been sick in bed and Griffith "abused her outrageously" – more newspaper shorthand – "and struck her a terrific blow in the face." Along with the divorce, Inez asked that the court legally restore her maiden name, Collins. The divorce, however, was apparently never granted. It didn't need to be; in another month Inez would be a widow.

November came, and with it the assault trial in Glenwood Springs. Even with his freedom on the line, Billy Griffith was unable, or unwilling, to restrain himself. He made it loudly and generally known that anyone who dared testify against him would pay, focusing particular rancor on Frank Sample, a New Castle real estate agent who was evidently the prosecution's main witness. On Tuesday, November 22, the court convicted Griffith of the vicious attack on John Pine. His attorney filed an immediate motion for a new trial, and the court scheduled a hearing on this motion for the following Monday. Meanwhile, despite the overt threats he'd made against Sample and others, Griffith was inexplicably freed on bond. He celebrated this minor win in true William Griffith style; he got stinking drunk.

Griffith was in no better shape the following day when he showed up back in New Castle. He continued to air his threats, not only against Sample but apparently against anyone who had ever crossed him. The *Grand Junction Daily Sentinel* later reported that "Griffith had been heard to say that he would 'get' Sample and a few more and would kill himself." Anybody familiar with Griffith would know that these were no idle words. Word spread around town that Griffith was looking for blood and one of those who heard tell of his dark threats was the town's current marshal, John Rennix.

From what followed, it appears that one of Griffith's first actions after stepping off the train from Glenwood Springs was to go to his room and arm himself. Either then, or at some later point, he also wrote a brief letter, sealed it in an envelope, and stuck it in his pocket. He hit the streets with two revolvers in his pockets and revenge on his mind. He walked to the railroad depot shared by the Colorado Midland and the Denver & Rio Grande. One of the persons on Griffith's enemies list, according to the *Denver Post*, was a black porter on the Midland line "against whom he has some real or imaginary grievance." Griffith had sworn to kill the man on sight, was here to make good, and was greatly annoyed when he learned the gent was out on a run and wouldn't be back until after dark. He stalked away muttering racial epithets and promising he'd settle with the porter in due time.

One plan frustrated, Griffith moved on to the next. First he would attend to business of another sort. Leila McMichael was sitting in a restaurant, also located in the Trimble building, when Griffith appeared. He dropped the sealed letter in her lap, said, "Keep this, it may do you some good," and left as abruptly as he'd entered. It's unclear whether McMichael read the letter then or later. If she read it then, she surely saw what his plan was – if she didn't already know. In any case, she wouldn't have to wait long to find out.

Not five minutes after delivering his letter, Griffith spotted Frank Sample walking down the opposite side of the street. It was the chance he'd been waiting for. He confronted and began berating the real estate man, trying to goad him into a fight. Marshal Rennix, who had been keeping tabs on Griffith in hopes of heading off trouble, saw the two talking and moved toward them. He reached the pair just as Griffith boasted that he had a gun and would allow Sample to go home and get one, because he didn't want to shoot an unarmed man. Hoping to defuse the hot situation, Rennix laid a friendly hand on Griffith's shoulder and said, "Billy, just put up your gun for we are not going to have any trouble here." Griffith's reply was quick and brutal. He pulled one of his pistols and snapped two close range shots at the marshal. One missed; the other did not, and Rennix fell with a bullet in his groin. Fearing he would be next, Sample fled, and

Griffith pursued him down the street, firing wildly as he ran. Rennix, meanwhile, was still in the fight. He raised himself with one arm, took steady aim and shot Griffith. The bullet hit his assailant in the meat under his left arm. It was a flesh wound, but painful, and was enough to cause Griffith to fall and allow Frank Sample to get away. Griffith got to his feet, but abandoned his chase. Instead, he sprinted for the Trimble building and ducked inside. A passerby would later find Griffith's second pistol, fully loaded, lying where he'd lost it when he fell.

People on the street who had seen and heard the shooting may have thought the worst was over. If so, they were mistaken. While Rennix was being carried off to a doctor, Griffith was heading upstairs to his quarters to put the final, fatal part of his muddled plan into action. Leila McMichael was still in the restaurant and Griffith called to her from the staircase, "Good-by, little girl. I've left you all I have." If she hadn't read his letter yet, it's a safe bet she did it then. Griffith rushed up to his room, forted up with a Winchester rifle, and took a vantage point at the window, scanning the main street below. Whether he was sober enough by now to realize the fix he was in, or this had been his aim all along, is impossible to say. Either way, he surely knew he would have to answer for shooting Rennix. Someone would be coming.

Down the street, some fifteen minutes later, came Will Davis – an affable coal miner in his late twenties with a wife and a seven-year-old daughter. Like Griffith, he was of Welsh descent. Like Griffith he was carrying a Winchester rifle. But unlike Griffith, he wasn't looking to shoot anyone. Davis had borrowed the rifle from a friend in town for a hunting trip, and he was returning it now, blissfully unaware of Griffith's mad rampage. As Davis neared the corner of Third and Main thinking of anything but death, a shot rang out from Griffith's window. Whether from fear that the rifle-toting miner was gunning for him, or out of pure mad-dog meanness, Griffith had seen his shot and taken it. As the *Grand Junction Daily Sentinel* bluntly put it, "Davis fell dead with the top of his head blown off."

Philip Henry Carpenter, who ran a local restaurant with his wife, saw Davis fall. The sight was doubly shocking; Will Davis was his son-in-law. Reports vary on what the 59-year-old café man did next. Some accounts say he tried to drag Davis' body to safety, while others say he hoisted Davis' fallen Winchester for a shot at Griffith. What is certain is that the man barricaded in the Trimble building fired again. Griffith's slug tore into Carpenter's left shoulder, smashing the bone and forcing him to seek cover.

1910 had not been not a good year for Philip and Jennie Carpenter. Five months earlier their daughter Libbie, the sister of Will Davis' wife, had shot and killed her husband during a bitter quarrel. The jury had acquitted Libbie, but now the Carpenters had lost a son-in-law and, according to early predictions, Philip might not survive his wound. It could have been coincidence, or the vengeful Griffith may have had another motive for sniping at Carpenter: Frank Sample, the prosecution witness, was a boarder in the Carpenters' home.

In any case, the mood on the streets of New Castle now took a dramatic turn. The initial shock and panic caused by Rennix's shooting and Griffith's promiscuous gunfire was past. With the cold-blooded murder of Davis and the wounding of Carpenter, the town's fear was turning to outrage. With his marshal out of action, the town's mayor, John W. Ritter, stepped forward. Citizens had already begun arming themselves; Ritter got them organized. He posted men with rifles covering every side of Griffith's building. He wisely ordered every saloon in town closed until further notice. He also summoned reinforcements, telephoning Glenwood Springs to speak with Mayor Edward E. Drach, himself a former New Castle resident. "All of Glenwood's firearms were brought out," the *Grand Junction Daily Sentinel* reported, "and a posse formed which started for New Castle as soon as a D & RG engine and caboose could be secured." Mayor Drach relayed word to Garfield County Sheriff P.W. Divelbiss, who was in Rifle, about fifteen miles southwest of New Castle. The sheriff started for the scene of the shootings straightaway. Garfield County coroner Dr. Granville Hopkins and Undersheriff Howard set off together from Glenwood Springs.

Back in New Castle, nerves were becoming frayed. As three hours dragged by with no sounds or signs of movement from the sniper's nest, the townsmen were getting edgy. The gory sight of Davis' body, still sprawled in the open where nobody dared break cover to approach it, didn't help. As night came on, Mayor Ritter ordered lights out in all the homes and businesses up and down Main Street. There was talk of setting the building afire to smoke Griffith out. Some even suggested dynamite. Ritter vetoed any such notions; help was on the way, and they would hold their ground until it arrived. Finally, the tension became too much for one of the men, and he decided to try for a lucky shot through Griffith's darkened window. This started "a regular bombardment," said the *Daily Sentinel*, "which did not end until 250 to 500 shots had been fired." The gratuitous gunfire managed to turn most of the paneling and trim in Griffith's room to kindling, but apart from that it accomplished nothing.

As 7 p.m. approached, Sheriff Divelbiss, his undersheriff riding with the coroner, and the special train carrying the Glenwood posse, all arrived within a few minutes' time. "Just as the sheriff arrived," wrote the *Steamboat Pilot*, "another fusillade was fired by citizens at the building," with similar results. Word immediately reached the sheriff that the posse might not be needed, that Griffith might already be dead. Leila McMichael, who had remained downstairs in the Trimble building throughout the entire ordeal, claimed that fifteen to twenty minutes after Griffith shot Carpenter, she had heard a single, muffled gunshot coming from his room, followed by a thud, as though a body had fallen.

The lawmen weren't quite sure how to act on this information. McMichael was not exactly an impartial source, and nobody was anxious to go poking his head through Will Griffith's doorway. It was the woman herself who settled it. If the officers would accompany her up the stairs, Leila McMichael offered, she would go to Griffith's room and check. He wasn't going to shoot her.

With no better plan at hand, Sheriff Divelbiss agreed. The sheriff and a couple of men, along with a neighbor named Mrs. Van Luven – apparently for moral support – cautiously followed McMichael up the stairway. When she reached Griffith's door, she gave it a light tap and called out, "It's I, Will. It's Leila." She received no reply, so she opened the door and went inside. As she walked across the dark room, trying to get her bearings, she stumbled against something heavy lying on the floor. It was as she'd expected; Griffith was stretched out on the floor, dead, a bullet through his head and his rifle lying underneath him. Divelbiss and the other men came in close behind McMichael. "The woodwork of the rooms [sic] was riddled with bullets," an Associated Press dispatch said, "one of which is thought to have killed him."

It appeared that the townsmen's volleys had found their target after all, until Dr. Hopkins inspected the body. The bullet had entered just over Griffith's right eye and exited out the top of his head. On examination,. Hopkins saw that Griffith's eyebrow was singed and his forehead powder burned. Suicide was so obvious that Hopkins deemed an inquest unnecessary. In Griffith's pocket was found the pistol, all chambers now empty, that he had used to shoot John Rennix.

Marshal Rennix, while all this was going on, had had his wound dressed and been made as comfortable as possible, but the bullet had perforated his intestines and he was in obvious and immediate need of surgery. Dr. Hopkins, along with serving as coroner, was also a well-known surgeon, and he took charge of the patient. Rennix was placed aboard the special train the posse had come in, and under the care of Drs. Hopkins, Stewart and Clark, he was taken to the Glenwood Springs sanatorium. There, the doctors found that Griffith's pistol bullet had perforated his lower intestine in five places. They removed fifteen inches of intestine but were unable to extract the lead slug, which had lodged against his spine. The marshal "rallied after the operation," reported an optimistic *Eagle Valley Enterprise*, and by the following day, "the hospital staff announced that he has a fighting chance for recovery."

The newspapers, meanwhile, took some satisfaction in announcing the ignominious end of Colorow. "Crazed with drink," the next day's *Denver Post* began, "...Will Griffith, a New Castle saloonkeeper, committed suicide to save himself from lynching at the hands of an angry mob." The *Telluride Journal* wrote, with a surplus of commas, that "New Castle celebrated with a Thanksgiving Eve murder, William Griffith, who graduated from the baseball diamond to a saloonkeeper, Wednesday night shooting, killing a coal miner by the name of Will Davis."

The news from Glenwood Springs was far more somber on November 25, two days after the shootings. Despite the hopeful prognosis, John Morgan Rennix died just before noon. His wife, Eva, and his daughters were at his bedside. Before he died, he made a statement that Billy Griffith had shot him "absolutely without provocation and that he was glad the saloonkeeper had committed suicide, for he surely would have been lynched by the marshal's friends." It's a strong example of John Rennix's character that on his deathbed he had thoughts of mercy for his killer.

In publishing the tragic news, the Colorado press was not nearly as charitable. "That Griffith had made careful plans for wholesale murder," stated the *Colorado Springs Gazette*, "is indicated by a letter given to his sweetheart just before the shooting on Wednesday." Below this, the *Gazette* printed the brief contents of Griffith's mysterious sealed envelope verbatim. Equal parts manifesto, suicide note and last will and testament, it read as follows:

"New Castle, Colo., Nov. 23 –

SALOON MAN KILLS ONE, WOUNDS ONE, COMMITS SUICIDE

Barricaded Himself in Room After Running Amuck and Shoots From Window.

TOWN MARSHAL A HERO

Receives Bullet Intended for Another and Is Probably Fatally Injured.

The *Denver Post* gave Marshal Rennix proper credit for saving Frank Sample from being murdered. The next day's *Post* would carry the sad news that his heroism had cost the lawman his own life. *(Author's Collection)*

I hereby certify that I have said and stated that I will have revenge on any man that I can see that has convicted me on a charge I was not guilty of. Anything in my possession goes to Leila McMichael. Please see that it does the same."

The letter bore Griffith's signature underneath, appended with, *"The writer of this letter, 'COLOROW'."*

To the end, Griffith was clearly proud of his fearsome moniker. But there was no pride, and certainly no sympathy, expressed for Colorow. His record and his actions spoke for themselves.

On November 26, The *Democrat-Times* in Aspen, where he had once been an admired athletic celebrity of sorts, printed a blistering editorial condemning the courts for granting Griffith bail and allowing the tragedy at New Castle. "Again is our attention called to the laxity of Colorado's law and once more are we compelled to chronicle another black crime on this state." And chronicle it did; the paper detailed Griffith's violent history, going back to the shooting of Mayor Norris, and characterized his beating of John Pine in April as "one of the most fiendish assaults ever made on a human being." It mentioned

Griffith's known reputation as a "gun man" and the threats he had made concerning his trial, pointing out despite all this, "the law permits such a dangerous man at large, in fact, gives him a permit to go and 'get' those whom he had threatened." The article wound down by expressing the opinion that it was "too bad that the judge or process of law granting 'Colorow' his liberty cannot be made to forever take care of the wives and children who have lost their support."

A news dispatch from Glenwood Springs the day of Rennix's death was perhaps his most fitting eulogy. It said, "John M. Rennix, the city marshal of Newcastle [sic], died here this morning, a martyr to duty. Rennix stopped the wild career of William Griffith, alias 'Colorow', the saloonkeeper who went on a rampage Wednesday, killing one man and wounding another, and who was himself shot to death a short time later."

In all the outpouring of sorrow and anger over Rennix's murder, Griffith's other victims were not forgotten. Fears were expressed that Carpenter would succumb to his wound. "The bullet shattered Carpenter's shoulder," the *Denver Post* said on the 27th, "and blood poisoning may develop." The following week the *Eagle Valley News* claimed that Carpenter was "reported to be dying." Records are vague as to whether this proved to be the case. Carpenter's grave marker in New Castle's Highland Cemetery lists no date, or place, of death. A 1911 business directory for New Castle offers one small clue; it carries a listing for "Home Restaurant, Mrs. P. H. Carpenter, Prop."

Both John Rennix and William J. Davis had been members of the Grand River Lodge of the New Castle International Order of Odd Fellows, and the lodge saw to both of their funerals. Both were buried in Highland Cemetery; Davis on the 26th and Rennix the following day. On the 28th, a joint memorial service for the men was held at the Methodist Church in New Castle, "and even this building," the *Eagle*

County Blade noted, "was too small to permit the many friends to get inside."

Griffith's brother, John, was located in Butte, Montana, and informed of his death. He requested that the body be held until he could come out on the train. Once John Griffith arrived, his brother's funeral was held in New Castle at Hahn's Opera House. There are no news reports of overflow crowds; if the opera house was packed, it was more likely with morbid gongoozlers than the sincerely bereaved. Afterward, William Griffith was also laid to rest in Highland Cemetery. Though this may have stuck in the craw of the victims' families, a generous soul like John Rennix likely wouldn't have cared at all.

There is no record of whether Leila McMichael ever collected – or tried to – on the "will" that Griffith left behind. It's doubtful she could have, since he died with his divorce pending. It's unlikely that a ne'er-do-well like Griffith had left much worth claiming anyway.

For reasons unknown, though he rests next to his first wife, Lieuvernia May, John Rennix was buried in an unmarked grave. In July of 2009, the New Castle town council corrected this, honoring its former marshal with a dignified headstone done in the same style as May's.

One hundred and twenty years before that, the coal fire deep below Ward's Peak started, prompting locals to dub the peak "Burning Mountain." It was burning when John Rennix moved to New Castle, burning when he died there, and it burns still. It might be viewed as a sort of tribute to the fallen marshal, this "eternal flame." He wouldn't expect such an honor – men like him never do – but he would be proud to share it with those brave souls who came before and after, and who gave their all. For that's the mark of a true hero.

Bibliography

Chapter 1- Symons

Newspapers
Daily Nevada State Journal, 1878-1886
Nevada State Journal, 1937-1951
Reno Evening Gazette, 1879 -1945
Weekly Reno Gazette, 1879-1880

Books
Bicknell, Charles F. and Thomas P. Hawley. *Reports of Cases Determined in the Supreme Court of the State of Nevada, During 1880; Volume 15.* San Francisco: A.L. Bancroft and Company, 1881.

Clark, Walter Van Tilburg, editor. *The Journals of Alfred Doten 1849-1903. Volume 1.* Reno: University of Nevada Press, 1973.

De Quille, Dan (William Wright). *History of the Big Bonanza.* San Francisco: A.L. Bancroft and Company, 1877.

Statutes of the State of Nevada Passed at the Thirteenth Session of the Legislature, 1887.
Carson City: State Printing, 1887.

Wren, Thomas. *A History of the State of Nevada: Its Resources and People.* New York: Lewis Publishing Company, 1904.

Public Records
1870 United States Census - Gold Hill, Storey County, Nevada
1880 United States Census - Carson City, Ormsby County, Nevada
1880 United States Census - Gold Hill, Storey County, Nevada

1900 United States Census - Gold Hill, Storey County, Nevada
1920 United States Census - Gold Hill, Storey County, Nevada
1930 United States Census - Gold Hill, Storey County, Nevada
1940 United States Census - Gold Hill, Storey County, Nevada
Nevada State Library and Archives: Nevada State Prison Inmate
Case Files

Chapter 2 - Hollister

Newspapers
Arkansas City Traveler, 1882-1884
Atchison Globe, 1883
Caldwell Commercial, 1883
Caldwell Journal, 1883-1884
Caldwell Post, 1879
Dodge City Times, 1884
Helena (Montana) Independent, 1883
Kansas City Daily Journal, 1897
Lawrence Journal, 1884
New York Times, 1883
Sedalia (Missouri) Weekly Bazoo, 1884
Vinita (Indian Territory) Indian Chieftain, 1884
Wichita Daily Eagle, 1884-1896
Winfield Courier, 1882-1884

Books
Jackson, Mary E. *The Life of Nellie C. Bailey, or A Romance of the West.* Topeka, R.E. Martin and Company, Printers and Binders, 1885.

Miller, Nyle H. and Joseph W. *Why the West Was Wild.* Norman, Oklahoma: University of Oklahoma Press, 1963.

Ridings, Sam P. *The Chisholm Trail: A History of the World's Greatest Cattle Trail.* Guthrie, Oklahoma: Co-operative Publishing Company, 1936.

Robertson, Alexander. *Madcap Nellie, A Novel in Real Life.* Chicago: Donohue and Henneberry, 1888.

Public Records
1870 United States Census – Milford Township, Knox County, Ohio
1880 United States Census – City of Caldwell, Sumner County, Kansas
1900 United States Census – Valley Township, Canadian County,
Oklahoma Territory

Chapter 3 - Gosling

Newspapers
Cheyenne Daily Leader, 1882
Chicago Daily Tribune, 1885
Dallas Morning News, 1886-1903
Dallas Southern Mercury, 1903
Fort Worth Daily Gazette, 1885-1887
Galveston Daily News, 1882-1904
Kansas City Times, 1885
New York Sun, 1904
New York Times, 1877-1904
San Antonio Daily Express, 1886-1898
San Antonio Daily Light, 1885-1900
San Antonio Evening Light, 1882
San Antonio Express, 1904-1930
San Antonio Light, 1884-1931
Weimar Mercury, 1885
Wise County Messenger, 1885

Books
Barnes, Charles Merritt. *Combats and Conquests of Immortal Heroes.* San Antonio: Guessaz and Ferlet Company, 1910.

Bronson, Edgar Beecher. *The Red-Blooded Heroes of the Frontier.* New York: George H. Doran Company, 1910.

Corner, William. *San Antonio de Bexar: A Guide and History.* San Antonio: Bainbridge and Corner, 1890.

Daniel, L.E. *Personnel of the Texas State Government, with Sketches of Distinguished Texans.* Austin: Press of the City Printing Company, 1887.

Edwards, Henry. *A History of the Texas Press Association.* Dallas: Southwestern Printing Company, 1916.

Hardin, John Wesley. *The Life of John Wesley Hardin.* Seguin, Texas: Smith and Moore, 1896.

Jackson and Jackson. *Reports of Cases Argued and Appealed in the Court of Appeals of Texas, Volume XIII.* Austin: Hutchings Printing House, 1887.

McRaven, William Henry. *Nashville, Athens of the South.* Nashville: Tennessee Book Company, 1949.

Roberts, Dan W. *Rangers and Sovereignty.* San Antonio: Wood Printing and Engraving Company, 1914.

Swindells, Eugene W. *A Legislative Manual for the State of Texas.* Austin: Published by E.W. Swindells, 1883.

United States Naval Academy. *Annual Register of the United States Naval Academy at Annapolis. MD. for the Academic Year 1867-'68.* Washington, D.C.: Government Printing Office, 1867.

Periodicals
Beseler, Ernest. "The Killing of Hal Gosling in 1885." *Frontier Times.* February, 1924: 20-22.
"Colonel Will Lambert." *The Inland Printer. Volume IX, Number 1.* October, 1891: 64-65.
Hunter, J. Marvin, Sr. "Early Day Stage Robbers." *Frontier Times.* January, 1947: 293-295.
Public Records
1880 United States Census – Castroville, Medina County, Texas

Chapter 4 - Gilley

Newspapers

Atchison Daily Globe, 1889

Chicago Tribune, 1885-1889

Hutchinson News, 1895

Kansas City Star, 1885-1910

Kansas City Times, 1885-1889

Kansas City Journal, 1895

Lawrence Daily Journal, 1899

New York Times, 1888-1889

Rocky Mountain Daily News (Denver), 1889

Sedalia (Missouri) Weekly Bazoo, 1889

St. Louis Republic, 1889

Topeka Daily Capital, 1889

Topeka Weekly Capital, 1889

Wichita Daily Eagle, 1889

Books

Andreas, Alfred Thayer and William G. Cutler. *History of the State of Kansas.* Chicago: A.T. Andreas Western Historical Publishing Company, 1883.

Gould's 1908 City Directory for the Greater Kansas City Area. Kansas City: Gould Publishing Company, 1908.

Morgan, Perl W. *History of Wyandotte County Kansas and its People, Volume II.* Chicago: The Lewis Publishing Company, 1911.

Wyandotte County and Kansas City, Kansas. Chicago: The Goodspeed Company, 1890.

222

Periodicals
Taylor, Loren. "The Death of Detective John W. Gilley." *The Historical Journal of Wyandotte County, Volume 1, Number 2.* Winter, 2001: 62-65.

Public Records
1885 Kansas State Census – Wyandotte County, Kansas
1860 United States Census – Springfield City, Clark County, Ohio
1870 United States Census – Ottawa City, Franklin County, Kansas
1880 United States Census – Ottawa, Franklin County, Kansas
1900 United States Census – Kansas City, Wyandotte County, Kansas
1910 United States Census – Council Grove, Morris County, Kansas
1920 United States Census – Franklin County, Kansas
1920 United States Census – St. Louis, Missouri
1930 United States Census – Ottawa, Franklin County, Kansas

Chapter 5 - Isbell

Newspapers
Brenham Weekly Banner, 1879
Dallas Morning News, 1888-1892
Fort Worth Daily Gazette, 1890-1892
Galveston Daily News, 1892
McKinney Democrat, 1892
National Police Gazette, 1879
New York Sun, 1879
New York Times, 1891
San Antonio Daily Light, 1892
Sherman Daily Register, 1887-1892
Velasco Daily Times, 1892

Books
Johnson, Frank W., et al. *A History of Texas and Texas, Volume III.*
Chicago and New York: The American Historical Society, 1914.

Loughery, E.H. *Texas State Government, A Volume of Biographical Sketches and Passing Comment.* Austin: MacLeod and Jackson, Printers, 1897.

White, John P. *The Texas Criminal Reports. Cases Argued and Adjudged in the Court of Criminal Appeals of the State of Texas. Volume 31.* Austin: State of Texas, 1893.

Public Records
1870 United States Census – Goshen Precinct, Warren County, Kentucky
1880 United States Census – Grayson County, Texas

Chapter 6 - Bogard

Newspapers
Berkeley Gazette, 1895
Fresno Bee, 1895
Fresno Morning Republican, 1885-1913
Fresno Republican Weekly, 1895
Los Angeles Herald, 1895
Los Angeles Times, 1895-1896
New York Times, 1895
Oakland Tribune, 1895-1936
Red Bluff Sentinel, 1893
Reno Weekly Gazette and Stockman, 1895
Sacramento Bee, 1905-1911
Sacramento Record-Union, 1895
Salt Lake Tribune, 1895
Salt Lake Herald, 1895
San Francisco Call, 1893-1904
San Francisco Chronicle, 1895-1896
San Francisco Morning Call, 1893
San Jose Mercury News, 1895
Washington Post, 1895-1913
Weekly Nevada State Journal, 1895
Woodland Daily Democrat, 1895-1898

Books
Delay, Peter. *History of Yuba and Sutter Counties, California.* Los Angeles: Historic Record Company, 1924.

Duke, Thomas S. *Celebrated Criminal Cases of America.* San Francisco: James H. Barry Company, 1910.

King, Ernest La Marr and Robert E. Mahaffay. *Main Line: Fifty Years of Railroading with the Southern Pacific.* New York: Doubleday, 1948.

Palm, Charles W. *California Attorneys Directory; Also Containing Complete List of All County Officers and Justices of the Peace in the State of California, and State Officers.* Los Angeles: Charles W. Palm Company, 1897.

Parkinson, R.R. *Pen Portraits: Autobiographies of State Officers, Legislators, Prominent Business and Professional Men of the Capital of the State of California.* San Francisco: Alta California Print, 1878.

Pinkerton, William Allen. *Train Robbery, Train Robbers, and the Holdup Men.* Chicago and New York: William A. and Robert A. Pinkerton, 1907.

The Statutes of California and Amendments to the Codes. Sacramento: A.J. Johnson, Superintendent State Printing, 1897.

Willis, William L. *History of Sacramento County, California.* Los Angeles: Historic Record Company, 1913.

Periodicals
Black, Jack. "What's Wrong with the Right People?" *Harper's Monthly Magazine.* June, 1929: 75-82.

Public Records
1880 California Voter Register, Tehama County
1880 United States Census – Tehama, Tehama County, California

Chapter 7 – Cameron, Koch, Lerri, White and Woodsum

Newspapers
Berkeley Gazette, 1895
Daily Alta California, 1885-1886
Fresno Morning Republican, 1898
Hayward Review, 1898
Los Angeles Herald, 1898-1899
Los Angeles Times, 1898-1903
New York Times, 1898
Oakland Tribune, 1895-1944
Reno Evening Gazette, 1898
Sacramento Daily Record-Union, 1885-1898
San Diego Evening Tribune, 1898
San Francisco Call, 1895-1913
San Francisco Chronicle, 1898
Washington Post, 1898

Books
Baker, Joseph E. *Past and Present of Alameda County, California. Volume I.* Chicago: The S.J. Clarke Publishing Company, 1914.

Board of Supervisors. *San Francisco Municipal Reports for the Fiscal Year 1897-98, Ending June 30, 1898.* San Francisco: The Hinton Printing Company, 1898.

Calderwood, G.W. and G.T. Loofbourow. *Oakland - "Athens of the Pacific".* Oakland: G.T. Loofbourow and Company, 1896.

Husted, F.M. *Husted's Alameda, Oakland and Berkeley Directory for the Year 1903.* Oakland: F.M. Husted Directory Company, 1903.

Husted, F.M. *Husted's Alameda, Oakland and Berkeley Directory for the Year 1911.* Oakland: F.M. Husted Directory Company, 1911.

Michie, Thomas J. *American and English Corporation Cases. Volume XVI.* Charlottesville, Virginia: The Michie Company, 1902.

The Pacific Reporter. Volume 167. St. Paul, Minnesota, West Publishing Company, 1918.

The Penal Code of the State of California. San Francisco: A.L. Bancroft and Company, 1874.

Pomeroy, C.P. *Reports of Cases Determined in the Supreme Court of the State of California. Volume 138.* San Francisco: Bancroft-Whitney Company, 1903.

Shuck, Oscar T. *History of the Bench and Bar in California.* Los Angeles: The Commercial Printing House, 1901.

Whiting, Randolph V. *Reports of Cases Determined in the District Courts of Appeal of the State of California. Volume 34.* San Francisco: Bancroft-Whitney Company, 1918.

Whiting, Randolph V. *Reports of Cases Determined in the District Courts of Appeal of the State of California. Volume 41.* San Francisco: Bancroft-Whitney Company, 1921.

Periodicals

Jackson, Edwin R. "The Havoc Wrought by One Man." *Wide World Magazine. Volume II, Number 10.* January, 1899: 504-508.

Hammerton, Cecil. "The City of Oaks." *Overland Monthly.* January-
June 1896: 674-704

Public Records

1896 California Voter Register, Berkeley, Alameda County

1896 California Voter Register, Brooklyn Township, Fruitvale Precinct,
Alameda County

1896 California Voter Register, City of Oakland, Second Ward,
Alameda County

1896 California Voter Register, City of Oakland, Sixth Ward, Alameda
County

1896 California Voter Register, Oakland Township, Temescal Precinct,
Alameda County

1896 California Voter Register, Washington Township, Centerville
Precinct, Alameda County

1898 California Voter Register, Cancellations, Second Ward (Death),
Alameda County

1898 California Voter Register, Cancellations, Washington Township
(Death), Alameda County

1898 California Voter Register, City of Oakland, Second Ward,
Alameda County

1898 California Voter Register, City of Oakland, Seventh Ward,
Alameda County

1880 United States Census – San Francisco, San Francisco County,
California

1900 United States Census – Brooklyn Township, Alameda County,
California

1900 United States Census – Oakland, Alameda County, California

1910 United States Census – Oakland Township, Alameda County,
California

1900 United States Census – San Francisco, San Francisco County,
California

Chapter 8 – Dillingham

Newspapers
Cape Girardeau Democrat, 1900
Chicago Tribune, 1900
Dallas Morning News, 1900
El Paso Daily Herald, 1900
Guthrie (Oklahoma) Daily Leader, 1900
Holt County Sentinel, 1899
Hutchinson (Kansas) Daily News, 1898-1900
Kansas City Daily Journal, 1896
Kansas City Journal, 1896-1899
Kansas City Star, 1898-1900
Kansas Semi-Weekly Capital, 1900
Kinsley (Kansas) Graphic, 1900
Lawrence (Kansas) Daily World, 1897
Moberley Evening Democrat, 1900
Moberley Monitor-Index, 1935-1939
Nebraska State Journal, 1900
New York Times, 1900-1935
St. Genevieve Fair Play, 1897
St. Louis Republic, 1900
Wichita Daily Eagle, 1900

Books
History of Clay and Platte Counties, Missouri. St. Louis: National Historical Company, 1885.

Lesueur, Alexander A. *Official Manual of the State of Missouri. for the Years 1899-1900.* Jefferson City: Tribune Printing Company, 1899.

Paxton, W.M. *Annals of Platte County, Missouri.* Kansas City: Hudson-Kimberly Publishing Company, 1897.

Rader, Perry S. *Reports of Cases Determined by the Supreme Court of the State of Missouri. Volume 143.* Columbia, Missouri: E.W. Stephens, 1895.

Shackleford, D.W. *The Missouri Criminal Code, Indexed and Annotated.* Columbia, Missouri: E.W. Stephens, 1895.

The Southwestern Reporter. Volume 53. St. Paul, Minnesota: West Publishing Company, 1900.

United States Civil Service Commission. *Official Register of the United States 1943.* Washington: GPO, 1943.

Williams, Walter. *A History of Northwest Missouri. Volume III.* Chicago and New York: The Lewis Publishing Company, 1915.

Periodicals
"The Keeley Cure." *The Kansas City Medical Record. Volume IX, Number 5.* May, 1892: 185.

Simmons, George H., M.D. "Medical News." *The Journal of the American Medical Association. Volume XXXV.* July-December, 1900: 564.

Public Records
1900 United States Census, Carroll Township, Platte County, Missouri
1900 United States Census, Lee Township, Platte County, Missouri
1920 United States Census, Carroll Township, Platte County, Missouri
1930 United States Census, Carroll Township, Platte County, Missouri

1940 United States Census, Carroll Township, Platte County, Missouri
State of Missouri, Division of Health; Death Certificate: Henry L.
Dillingham
State of Missouri, Platte County; Marriage Certificate: Sterling P.
Harrington, Mary E. Wallace
State of Missouri, Platte County; Marriage Certificate: John W. Farley,
Emma S. Wallace
State of Washington, King County; Marriage Certificate: Jesse E.
Wright, Maude Harrington

Chapter 9 – Calhoun

Newspapers

Anti Horse Thief Association Weekly News, 1902
Atlanta Constitution, 1905
Daily Ardmoreite (Indian Territory), 1905
Daily Oklahoma State Capital, 1896
Emporia Gazette, 1905
Fort Worth (Texas) Star Telegram, 1905
Goodland Republic, 1893
Hays Free Press, 1905
Hutchinson News, 1899-1905
Iola Daily Register, 1899-1905
Kansas City Daily Journal, 1896-1899
Kansas City Star, 1899-1905
Kinsley Graphic, 1894
Lawrence Daily World, 1893
Los Angeles Herald, 1905
Manning (South Carolina} Times, 1894
Oakland (California) Tribune, 1905
Oklahoma State Capital, 1901-1905
Palestine (Texas) Daily Herald, 1905
New York Times, 1893-1905
New York Weekly Press, 1894
St. Paul (Minnesota) Daily Globe, 1893
Sedan Times, 1881
Sedan Lance, 1905
Vinita (Oklahoma Territory) Indian Chieftain, 1899
Wichita Daily Eagle, 1902

Books

Bartlett, C. *Dawn of the Twentieth Century: Cedar Vale, Kansas.* Cedar Vale, Kansas: Jones and Bartlett, 1901.

Case, Nelson. *History of Labette County, Kansas.* Chicago: Biographical Publishing Company, 1901.

Dodge, Fred and Carolyn Lake. *Under Cover for Wells Fargo: The Unvarnished Recollections of Fred Dodge.* Boston: Houghton Mifflin, 1969.

Galena, Kansas City Directory, Kansas City: Hoye Directory Company, 1900.

Standard Atlas of Chautauqua County, Kansas. Chicago: George A. Ogle and Company, 1903.

Tenth Biennial Report of the Directors, Wardens and Other Officers of the Kansas State Penitentiary. Topeka: The Kansas State Printing Company, 1896.

Periodicals

"Killed at His Post." *Express Gazette: The Official Journal of the Express Service of America. Volume XVIII, Number 9.* September 15, 1893: 198.

"Our Service Inspectors." *Santa Fe Magazine. Volume XV, Number 1.* December, 1920: 63-64.

"Women's Service on Railroads Studied." *The Bulletin: Issued by the Southern Pacific Company Bureau of News. Volume VIII, Number 12.* December, 1919: 10.

Public Records
1895 Kansas State Census, Burrton, Harvey County
1870 United States Census, Mound City Township, Linn County, Kansas
1880 United States Census, City of Sedan, Chautauqua County, Kansas
1880 United States Census, Clark Township, Wright County, Missouri
1900 United States Census, Burrton Township, Harvey County, Kansas
1900 United States Census, Cedar Vale, Chautauqua County, Kansas
1900 United States Census, Clark Township, Wright County, Missouri
1900 United States Census, Galena, Cherokee County, Kansas
1900 United States Census, Kansas State Penitentiary, Leavenworth County, Kansas
1900 United States Census, Summit Township, Chautauqua County, Kansas
1900 United States Census, Valley Township, Grant County, Oklahoma
1910 United States Census, Larned Township, Pawnee County, Kansas
1910 United States Census, Wichita, Sedgwick County, Kansas
1910 United States Census, Larned Township, Pawnee County, Kansas

Chapter 10 – Rennix

Newspapers
Aspen Daily Times, 1901
Aspen Democrat, 1904-1908
Aspen Democrat-Times, 1910
Aspen Tribune, 1901
Colorado Springs Gazette, 1910
Colorado Transcript, 1905
Denver Post, 1910
Eagle County Blade, 1910
Eagle Valley Enterprise, 1910
Fort Collins Courier, 1910
Glenwood Post, 1902
Grand Junction Daily Sentinel, 1910
Grand Valley News, 1910
Los Angeles Herald, 1910
Los Angeles Times, 1910
New Castle Nonpareil, 1901-1905
Steamboat Pilot, 1910
Telluride Journal, 1910

Books
Bird, Horace A. *History of a Line (Colorado Midland Railway).*
Denver; Passenger Department of the Colorado Midland Railway, 1889.

The Colorado State Business Directory. Denver: The Gazeteer
Publishing Company, 1911.

Gulliford, Andrew. *Garfield County, Colorado: The First Hundred
Years 1883-1983.* Glenwood Springs: Grand Farnum Printing, 1983.

Hall, Frank. *History of the State of Colorado. Volume IV.* Chicago: The
Blakeley Printing Company, 1895.

Periodicals
"Marketing Late Crop Potatoes." *U.S. Department of Agriculture:
Farmers' Bulletin No. 1578.* February, 1929: 28.

Public Records
1870 United States Census - Clay Township, Randolph County,
West Virginia
1880 United States Census - New Interest District, Randolph County,
West Virginia
1900 United States Census – East New Castle, Garfield County,
Colorado
1900 United States Census – West New Castle, Garfield County,
Colorado
1910 United States Census - Butte, Silver Bow County, Montana
1910 United States Census – East New Castle, Garfield County,
Colorado
1910 United States Census – Glenwood Springs, Garfield County,
Colorado
1910 United States Census – West New Castle, Garfield County,
Colorado

ABOUT THE AUTHOR

J.R. Sanders is a native of Newton, Kansas, one of the original "wild and woolly" cowtowns. His deep interest in Old West history dates back to childhood visits with his family to the Dalton Gang hideout, Abilene, and Dodge City. He's made history presentations to schools, colleges, and historical societies all over Southern California, and for institutions such as the Autry Museum of the American West and the Huntington Library. He has worked both on-camera and behind the scenes on historical documentaries.

A former Southern California police officer, he has written public service spots for television broadcast, feature articles for a variety of publications including *Law & Order* and *Wild West Magazine*, and is the author of two previous books. He is an active member of the Western Writers of America and the Wild West History Association.

For more information, the author's website is www.jrsanders.com.

CPSIA information can be obtained
at www.ICGtesting.com
Printed in the USA
FFOW01n2218201213
2742FF

9 781938 628238